Steve Parish
PUBLISHING

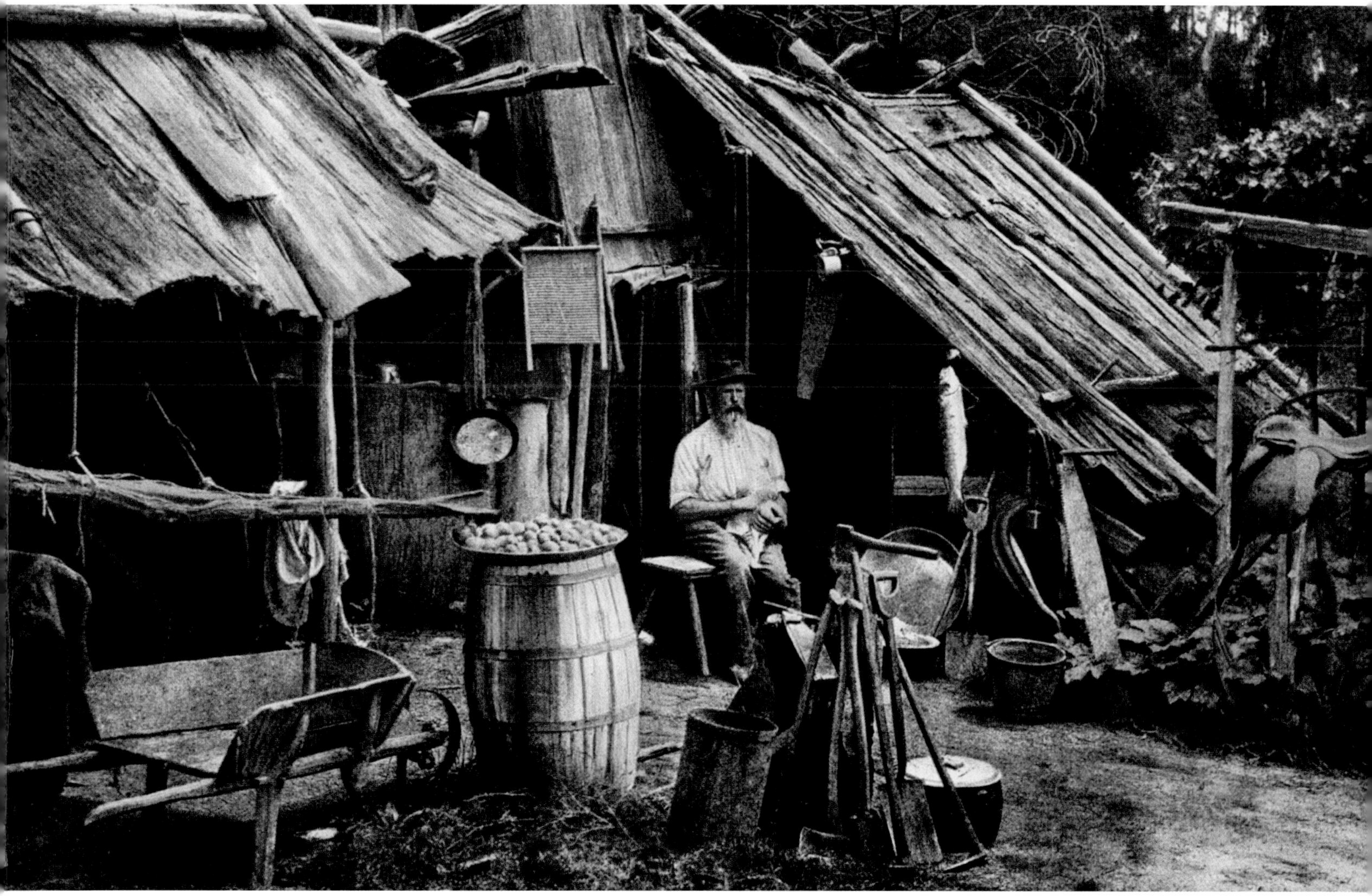

Amazing Facts about Australia's

Early Settlers

Author: Karin Cox
Principal Photographer: Steve Parish

AMAZING FACTS — AUSTRALIA'S EARLY SETTLERS

Contents

NED KELLY
Wanted For
MURDER
of Police near Mansfield

Above: **A recreated scene showing gold rush settlers at Sovereign Hill, Victoria.**

Australia's amazing early settlers

the FACTS!

SOME ABORIGINAL ROCK ART provides a visual representation of European explorers, depicting different customs and costumes.

NAVIGATOR WILLEM JANSZ and his crew did not realise they had found a new continent. Instead, they were convinced they had stumbled across part of New Guinea.

LATER, LUIZ VAEZ DE TORRES proved that the land was not part of New Guinea when he sailed the *San Pedrico* through what is now known as the Torres Strait. Unfortunately, his discovery remained secret for 150 years, further obscuring the true outline of the continent.

COMBINED, THE SHIPS of the First Fleet contained about the same number of people as three Boeing 747 plane loads.

BEFORE GOING ON BOARD the transport ship, each convict was given a medical examination. Once aboard they were assigned to a sleeping berth with 8–10 other convicts (these groups were known as a "mess"). Throughout the voyage, all members of one mess ate, slept, cooked and worked on deck at the same time, keeping the ships running in shifts.

TWENTY-THREE CONVICTS from the First Fleet died on the 36-week voyage to Botany Bay, including three females and twenty male convicts.

A BRIEF HISTORY OF DISCOVERY

Dutch, Spanish, Portuguese, French and British navigators began to discover the vast continent "down under" in the early 1600s. In 1606, Dutchman Willem Jansz became the first European known to sight Australian shores when he accidentally chanced upon the coast of the Gulf of Carpentaria in his ship, the *Duyfken*. More navigators followed, sailing names such as Luis Vaez de Torres, Abel Tasman and William Dampier right into the history books, but most paid little attention to the "great southern land" for more than a century. They believed that the rugged landscape they spied contained none of the riches sought after by burgeoning trading nations. On 22 August 1770, Briton Lieutenant (later Captain) James Cook claimed the east coast of Australia as British territory, naming it New South Wales. It wasn't until almost seven years later that the British began to see the potential of their newly discovered territory — as a continental prison for Britain's criminals and undesirables. At that time, they believed it to be a land largely devoid of inhabitants, a belief that we now know to be untrue. Antarctica aside, Australia was the last continent to be settled by Europeans. This fascinating, often formidable land has an equally harsh but interesting history. In little more than 200 years, Australia became the "lucky country" it is today — one nation cobbled together from brave Indigenous warriors, weary convicts, fortune seekers and courageous settlers determined to find a better life for their families.

Nationhood did not come easily. In the early days of settlement, those who called the newly "discovered" continent their home shed blood, sweat and tears. Indigenous Australians, the traditional owners for many thousands of years, suffered disease, displacement and death at the hands of the newcomers — many of whom suffered themselves, under the yoke of imprisonment. Settlers braved the elements and the isolation daily, engaging in back-breaking work in an attempt to "tame" or transform the resistant Australian bush into arable farmlands. Fortune-hunters drew strength from the possibility of riches untold, as they encountered the flies, heat, disease and violence of the goldfields. Many immigrants and Aborigines endured racial taunts, attacks or slavery; however, over time, all helped to change the face (and policies) of Australia to create the multicultural mix that comprises our nation today.

The landscape, too, changed with the needs of settlers — often detrimentally. Scrub was cleared, large, polluting cities sprang up, and introduced plants and animals (brought to Australia by well-meaning people) competed with native flora and fauna. Once-pristine habitats changed forever and many species were lost to history. However, life, laws, beliefs and morals were very different 200 years ago, and hindsight is a wonderful magnifying glass for the mistakes of history. Over the course of Australia's settlement, many grave errors were made — mistakes that impacted on the lives of both Aborigines and immigrants — but it is only today, with the benefit of hindsight, that we recognise them as such. In 1606, when Europeans first set foot on the Australian continent, and later, when they began to be transported to these shores or to migrate in search of prosperity, neither the Aborigines nor the settlers knew what the future would bring.

Left: **James Cook claimed Australia as British territory in 1770.**

Above: Convicts being deported.

Left: Far more men than women were sent out on the First Fleet, some of them leaving a wife and starving children back in Britain.

PRISON AT WORLD'S END

Britain already had a history of shipping criminals to other shores, mostly the "New World" of the Americas. However, following the end of the American War of Independence in 1783, American colonies would no longer tolerate British convicts. The industrial revolution in Britain meant that many people were out of work, because goods that were once made by hand were able to be produced quickly and cheaply by machines in factories. Towns and cities became overcrowded with unemployed, poverty-stricken people and petty crime and theft escalated.

With gaols and "hulks" (old, often decaying ships moored off cities) full to overflowing, the British Government needed somewhere to send convicted felons. Botany Bay, about 24,000 km away from Britain, seemed the perfect place. Joseph Banks and James Matra, who had both travelled on Cook's earlier voyage to New South Wales, suggested Botany Bay as a suitable site for a colony. Banks likened the Australian climate to the south of France and was sure convicts would be able to grow food and support themselves there, so, in August 1786, Britain's Pitt Government agreed to establish a penal colony at Botany Bay. Captain Arthur Phillip was commissioned as Governor in October 1786 and a fleet of eleven ships was assembled. The ships were the HMS *Sirius*, HMS *Supply, Alexander, Charlotte, Scarborough, Prince of Wales, Lady Penrhyn, Friendship, Borrowdale, Fishburn* and *Golden Grove* (the last three being supply vessels).

What happened WHEN?

50,000 YEARS AGO+ Aborigines first inhabit Australia.

1000 AD Macassans begin to visit Australian waters to gather Trepang (sea cucumber).

1606 Willem Jansz makes first known European landing on mainland.

1642–43 Abel Tasman discovers Australia and New Zealand.

1699 Englishman William Dampier spends three months on the coast of Western Australia.

1770 James Cook claims Australia for the British.

1788 Governor Arthur Philip and the First Fleet arrive to establish a penal colony at Botany Bay.

IN SEARCH OF A BETTER LIFE

In the 1700s and early 1800s, England was a harsh country for poor people. Many families struggled to survive in the industrial age, when there was no dole or benefits for the unemployed. Often the homeless turned to begging, pick-pocketing or prostitution. If convicted of these crimes, punishment was harsh. As well as the adults, about 30,000 orphaned children lived in poverty on London's streets by the 1850s, huddling together in dark alleys and lanes (known as rookeries) at night. Many of them turned to crime and were tried as adults and imprisoned in floating hulks before being sentenced to transportation to Australia. At the time, more than 200 crimes were punishable by death, although most people were sentenced to life imprisonment. Those convicted of stealing animals or other goods that were worth more than five shillings could be put to death. Trying to form a workers' union also meant a death sentence. Lesser crimes received the punishment of transportation, until it became seen as the lesser of two evils. By the early 1800s, the new colony was thriving and many of Europe's underprivileged thought they could do better in Australia than in England. Some convicted prisoners even shouted "Hurrah" when they heard they would be transported to Australia!

Aborigines
— the first Australians

Above: In the north of the continent, Arafura File Snakes are still a reliable food source for Aborigines and Torres Strait Islanders.

For many thousands of years, long before Europeans even guessed at the existence of a great southern continent, Aboriginal people lived in Australia. Scientists are unsure exactly when, or how, Aborigines first populated the continent, but the bones of an Aboriginal man found at Lake Mungo in New South Wales and nicknamed "Mungo Man" have been dated at around 40,000 years old.

ABORIGINES PROBABLY arrived in Australia sometime before that date, during the last Ice Age, when ice sheets may have joined Indonesia to South-East Asia. Recent DNA research suggests some Australian Aborigines may even have come to the continent from New Guinea.

Historians estimate that 300,000–750,000 Aborigines lived in Australia at the time of European settlement, but the exact figure will never be known. They probably lived in 500–900 separate tribes, or nations, each of which had 50–2000 members. More than 200 languages were spoken, many of which may have included several dialects.

Right: Australia's traditional owners are commemorated on the two dollar coin.

MANY NATIONS

Within their territory, Aborigines moved around semi-nomadically from season to season, making the most of the plants and animals available. When Aborigines remained in one spot for a while, or lived semi-permanently in one area, some tribes constructed *gunyahs* or *wurleys* — rough huts made of branches covered in stringybark (left). In some places, log huts were built and in cold areas Aborigines may have lived in caves and fashioned long cloaks of possum skin. Some tribes also made canoes out of hollow trees and constructed bags and nets for catching fish. Fire was very important to the survival of Aborigines in cold areas and they shared it with friends and enemies alike.

Aborigines have a spiritual connection to the land, and landforms are believed to be the physical representations of ancestral heroes and spirits. Each Aboriginal nation has its own Dreaming tales, which explain features of the group's territory, beliefs and ancestry. The stories describe the creation of the world and the way people in that Aboriginal nation should behave and relate according to Aboriginal tribal law. Special events and ceremonies, such as corroborees, honour the ancient ancestors and the places where their spirits reside.

ABORIGINAL PEOPLE are believed to have settled the Sydney region around 20,000 years ago. At the time of European settlement, historians estimate there were about 75,000 Aboriginal people in what is now New South Wales, including the Dharug, Eora, Tharawal and Ku-ring-gai peoples. Probably around 1000 Indigenous people depended on the waters of Sydney Harbour for fish and shellfish.

the FACTS!

EACH ABORIGINAL NATION occupied its own territory of 500–100,000 km^2. This area provided the people with resources for their survival, such as food; animal skins; materials to make shelter, clothing, tools and musical instruments; minerals (such as ochre for body painting and rock art); and medicine (mostly made out of native plants).

AROUND 10,000 YEARS AGO at the end of the Ice Age, rising sea levels isolated Tasmania and limited contact between Tasmanian Aborigines (the Palawa people) and mainland Aborigines.

TASMANIAN ABORIGINES had different hairstyles for different Aboriginal nations. Indigenous men and women of the east and west coasts shaved their heads, leaving only a ring of hair on the lower or upper skull. On other parts of the island, women's hair was short while men painted their heads with red ochre.

BECAUSE the men and women of the First Fleet were all fully clothed, and the men were clean-shaven, the Aborigines were often confused about the sex of the newcomers.

THE ABORIGINES were delighted with the European's iron hatchets and traded their best spears for them.

INDIGENOUS PEOPLES around Port Macquarie fashioned canoes out of stringybark and, while fishing, kept a fire burning in the canoe on a thick base of clay.

"POOR BLACKFELLOW, white men take Blackfellow's country and frighten him too" one Aborigine is reported to have said in 1844.

Above, left to right: George Robinson, a missionary, oversaw the relocation of Tasmanian Aborigines to offshore islands. Unfortunately, they all died of hunger and disease; Aborigines lit fires by using flint stones or rubbing sticks together.

INVASION & DISPLACEMENT

When the Europeans first began to explore the continent and make contact with the Aboriginal people, many Aborigines, like the Gamaraigal people of Sydney, at first believed that the white Europeans were the spirits of dead ancestors. Trinkets, such as mirrors, nails, tomahawks and clothes, were used by the Europeans on the First Fleet to help buy the Aborigines' favour. David Collins, later the judge-advocate of the new colony, wrote that the Aborigines "conducted themselves socially and peaceably … and by no means seemed to regard [the English] as enemies or invaders of their country and tranquillity". These friendly relations did not last long. Unfortunately, many of the Europeans believed themselves better than the Aboriginal people and wanted to make the Aborigines more "civilised". Captain Watkin Tench wrote, "Our first object was to win their affections and our next to convince them of the superiority we possessed, for without the latter, the former we knew would be of little importance". They believed that hard work and religion would transform the "natives" into members of English society. Some Aborigines began to work for fish sellers in Sydney, others enlisted as trackers for the police force or were paid in food and keep to guide explorers on their travels. Sometimes, Aborigines worked as labourers or domestic servants. One settler wrote:

> *The Aborigines have helped me with the maize harvest. They have worked hard and well. At the end of the day we reward them with a good feast of pumpkin and sugar which they love. At the end … we will give them the boilings from the sugar bag, and grog (which they call 'tumble down') and they will leave happily.*

Differences in the way food was obtained also caused rivalry between Aborigines and white Australians. European settlers cleared land to grow crops or farm livestock — a method that was incompatible with the Aboriginal lifestyle. Cleared pastoral land did not suit the native plants and animals that the Aborigines ate, thus driving them away. Aborigines whose traditional land had been taken from them had to find other ways to get food. Life was extremely difficult for those who had been displaced. Many were cut off from their culture, traditions or interactions with other Aboriginal nations, and they often came under attack by the white settlers — either unprovoked or in retaliation for attacking livestock or Europeans.

Above: Ceremonial body painting, dance and music is central to Aboriginal culture.

Disease and death

Aboriginal people had no immunity to European diseases. In 1789, a smallpox epidemic swept through the colony, killing more than half the Aborigines of Botany Bay, Sydney Harbour, the Hawkesbury River area and Broken Bay.

TOWARDS RECONCILIATION

Since the 1970s, efforts have been made toward reconciliation. In 1978, the *Aboriginal Land Rights (Northern Territory) Act* was passed, giving Aborigines freehold title to 249,000 km^2 of reserve land in the Northern Territory. In 1981, the Pitjantjatjara people received title to the North West Aboriginal Reserve and adjacent pastoral leases in South Australia, and in 1983 the Federal Government transferred title of Uluṟu–Kata Tjuṯa National Park to traditional Aṉangu (Bininj) owners. The *Mabo* decision in 1992 gave Aborigines traditional custodial rights to Crown Land and, in 1996, the *Wik* decision extended custodial rights to pastoral leases. The Australian Government's apology in 2008, was another step towards reconciliation for all Australians.

Above: John Alcott's depiction of ships of the First Fleet anchored in Sydney Cove in 1788.

Arrival of the First Fleet

The eleven ships of the First Fleet, carrying more than 1400 people, left Portsmouth in England on 13 May 1787. They arrived at Botany Bay from 18–20 December 1787; however, Captain Arthur Phillip found the site unsuitable and moved to Port Jackson (now better known as Sydney Harbour) to found the new colony.

ON SATURDAY 26 JANUARY (now celebrated annually as Australia Day) the officers of the First Fleet raised the Union Jack (bottom), toasted the health of the royal family and the new colony, fired their muskets and cheered the founding of the colony.

BUILDING A NEW LIFE

The first task was to establish the hallmarks of settlement. There was no suitable accommodation so convicts and officers slept in tents until more permanent dwellings could be built. Male convicts were ordered to begin constructing buildings soon after they landed, with some of the earliest projects being a hospital, wharves, stores, a church, soldiers' barracks and homes for the officers. The only convicts with any kind of experience were one brickmaker, five bricklayers, three plasterers, three carpenters and a stonemason. The rest were inexperienced for the task of carpentry or construction and many of the initial buildings collapsed. Some of the first flimsy huts were hastily constructed out of wattle-and-daub, which did not withstand the heavy summer storms. Buildings to house the convicts were last on the list and as a result some convict boys slept in a hollow tree for months while huts were being built!

To keep male and female convicts separated, female felons remained on the ships until Wednesday 6 February 1788. The following day, Governor Phillip addressed the convicts and told them that those attempting to escape or trying to get into the women's quarters would be shot immediately. Anyone attempting to steal food or animals would face severe punishment. Those who refused to work would be denied food. "Many of you are innate villains" he noted. Female convicts were set to work crushing oyster shells to make lime for cement. Because there were no convict quarters, Governor Phillip soon realised it was impossible to keep the male and female convicts separated, so he began to recommend marriage in the hope that it would keep some of the felons and prostitutes from debauchery.

the FACTS!

WHEN THE FIRST FLEET sailed into Port Jackson, Surgeon White wrote: *"Port Jackson I believe to be, without exception, the finest and most extensive harbour in the universe ... "*

LIMITED personal possessions were allowed on board the First Fleet, but some of the affluent "gentlemen convicts" (usually convicted for forgery or fraud) may have carried a few books, a writing set or a piece of jewellery. Most left with just the shirts on their backs.

THE SUPPLY SHIPS of the First Fleet carried goods to help establish the colony, such as 14,000 shovels, 40 wheelbarrows, 8000 fish hooks and 5448 panes of glass.

A FEMALE CONVICT named Mary Bolton gave birth to the colony's first baby, Joshua, on one of the transport ships as the First Fleet entered Botany Bay. Babies of convicts were free-born and were labelled as BC on the government "muster" (or census), which stood for Born in the Colony.

THE COLONY DID NOT have a very auspicious start — on the 6 February, during a huge storm, lightning struck a tree in the centre of the camp, which fell and killed five sheep and a pig.

ON SUNDAY 10 FEBRUARY 1788, the first marriages in the colony were conducted when Reverend Richard Johnson married five couples, including Mary and William Bryant. He also baptised three children.

CAPTAIN ARTHUR PHILLIP (right) was considered a kind and able leader with a difficult role to fulfil. He was a well-regarded naval officer who could speak several languages and had farming experience, making him the logical choice for the position. He was born in London in 1738 and, after joining the British Navy at seventeen, served in the Seven Years' War against France and again in the American War of Independence. During his reign as governor he was sympathetic to the Aboriginal people and to the convicts he commanded. During the scarce "starving time" in the colony's early years, Captain Phillip and his officers received the same rations as the convicts. He was also the first to use Aboriginal guides and befriended many Aborigines during his time as governor. When he became ill after being speared by a hostile Aborigine at Manly, he returned to England, taking the Aborigines Bennelong and Yemmerawannie with him.

FELONS AS FARMERS

Farming was another skill that was in short supply, which, coupled with the sandy soil and the fact that Sydney was experiencing a drought, made obtaining food difficult. Much of the livestock was reserved as breeding stock, so the only available food was the ships' stores (and those that weren't salted were rancid due to the long sea voyage). Colonists had to rely on strict rations supplemented by whatever native flora and fauna they could hunt or gather. Fish were plentiful and, in accordance with Aboriginal tradition, were shared with the Aboriginal people. Fresh fruit and vegetables were in short supply, so native herbs were used to prevent scurvy. The colonists hunted and ate Emus and kangaroos, which one convict described as "like mutton, but much leaner", as well as ducks and other birds.

THE STARVING TIME

Within nine months, food was so scarce that the *Sirius* (one of two large vessels left in the colony) had to be sent to South Africa for supplies. The ship returned with flour, salt pork, medicines and seeds of wheat and barley. Despite the supplies, by the end of the colony's second year, rations were again very low. The provisions and equipment Governor Phillip had requested from England in 1788 had still not arrived. Messages had to be sent to England by ship, meaning that a response could take up to fifteen months.

By 1 November 1789, the colony was facing starvation. Rations were reduced to two-thirds for "every Man, from the Governor to the Convict". Women's rations, which had been two-thirds of the men's previous rations, were not reduced because by this stage many of the women had children or were breastfeeding.

Unfortunately, before the *Sirius* could be sent for another supply run, it was wrecked off Norfolk Island, leaving just the small *Supply.* It was an enormous risk to send the *Supply* to Batavia to replenish the colony's food stores in April 1790, but one Governor Phillip felt forced to make. Luckily the *Supply* was not shipwrecked or the entire colony would have been marooned in the strange new continent! Despite the hardship, the struggling colony clung to life and Governor Phillip set about seeking suitable sites for farms nearby.

the **FACTS!**

NO PLOUGHS were brought out with the First Fleet and there were no draught horses, making sowing fields difficult. To make matters worse, only three men had farming experience — Governor Phillip, James Ruse and Henry Dodd.

GOVERNOR PHILLIP wrote back to Britain saying, "*I hope few convicts will be sent for one year at least, except carpenters, masons and bricklayers, or farmers who can support themselves and assist in supporting others ... If fifty farmers were sent out with their families they would do more in one year in rendering this colony independent of the mother country ... than a thousand convicts*".

RATIONS WERE SO LOW that Governor Phillip asked his dinner guests to bring their own bread.

SOME CONVICTS actually starved to death during what became known as "the starving time".

SICK CONVICTS (below) or colonists were tended to in a rudimentary hospital run by surgeon John White. The surgeon, appalled by the conditions, wrote to England for medical supplies, including blankets and sheets, writing "*the want of them makes ... observance and attention to cleanliness ... utterly impossible*". He also noted that "*constantly living on salt provisions without any possibility of a change, makes them more necessary than perhaps in any other quarter of the globe*".

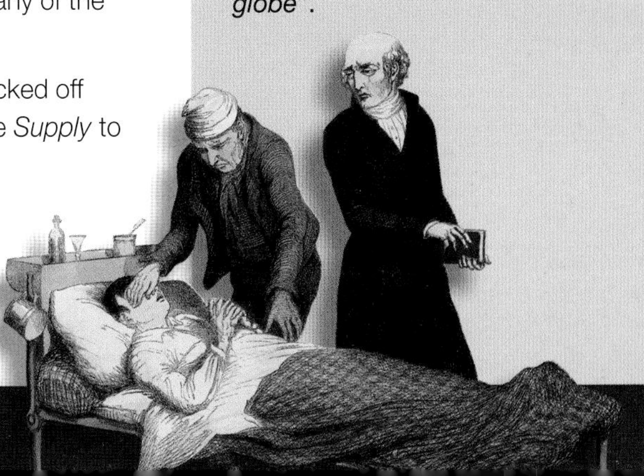

The death fleets

the FACTS!

BEFORE THE ARRIVAL of the Second Fleet, food was so scarce that for the theft of two cabbages, Private Richard Knight, a marine, was sentenced to 200 lashes. Another man, William Parr, who had stolen a pumpkin, received 500 lashes for his dishonesty. Joseph Elliot was sentenced to 300 lashes and loss of his flour ration for stealing potatoes, but had to have his rations reinstated or he would have starved to death.

BY 1 APRIL 1790, people in the colony were so weak from hunger that working hours were decreased to six hours a day.

ONE HUNDRED MEN OF THE NSW Corps, sent to help Phillip discipline the convicts, also arrived on the Second Fleet. They replaced the marines, who saw themselves as soldiers, not as jurors for criminals. Unfortunately, the NSW Corps were an unruly mob. Governor Hunter later wrote that some were "*superior in every species of infamy to the most expert in wickedness amongst the convicts*".

When another ship finally arrived on 3 June 1790, the ragged, starved prisoners, marines and officers of Sydney Cove wept with joy. It was the Lady Juliana *with a shipload of 222 female convicts on board. Four more ships of the Second Fleet arrived in 1790 and the eleven ships of the Third Fleet in 1791. Conditions on board these fleets were atrocious.*

BY THIS STAGE, the convicts and marines at the colony were all pitifully thin, but unfortunately, the store ship for the Second Fleet, *Guardian*, had been wrecked on an iceberg near the Cape of Good Hope. Consequently, the ships of the Second Fleet did not relieve the misery of the fledgling colony. In some ways they added to it, because the ships of the "Death Fleet", as the Second Fleet became known, carried many desperately ill convicts to Port Jackson.

ONLY FOUR CONVICTS DIED on the *Lady Juliana's* ten-month journey. However, when the three other convict ships of the Second Fleet struggled into the harbour from June 26–28 that same year, they had the worst death rate in all of the transportations to Australia. On board, more than 250 convicts had perished, mostly due to mistreatment by the officers; almost 500 more were desperately ill. These three ships — the *Surprize*, *Neptune* and *Scarborough* brought with them around 11,000 hungry convict mouths to feed. Mercifully, although the *Lady Juliana* carried few provisions, the next ship to arrive, *Justinian*, was laden with supplies. Reverend Richard Johnson, who witnessed the convicts of the Second Fleet disembarking wrote that, "Many were not able to walk, to stand, or to stir themselves in the least ... some creeped [sic] upon their hands and knees, and some were carried upon the backs of others". Later, in the hospital tent, he discovered that some were "covered over almost with their own nastiness, their heads, bodies, cloths [sic], blankets all full of filth and lice".

Below: Passengers on the *Lady Juliana* brought news that the store ship *Guardian* had been wrecked off the Cape of Good Hope (a tragedy recreated in this painting) leaving the colony at Port Jackson short of much-needed rations and equipment.

Above: The bridge leading to Bare Island, Botany Bay National Park.

BOUND FOR BOTANY BAY

Convict transportation to Australia lasted around 80 years from the First Fleet to the last transport, which arrived in Fremantle, Western Australia on 9 January 1868. All up, approximately 158,829 convicts were sentenced to transportation to Australia — of these, 134,261 were male and 24,468 were female and the rest were children. Most of them were English or Welsh (70%) although others were Irish (24%) or Scottish (5%). Some had also spent time in British colonies such as India and Canada. The remaining 1% was made up of Maoris, people from the Carribean (the first bushranger John Caesar, also known as Black Caesar, was born in the West Indies), and Chinese people from Hong Kong. Some were soldiers that were transported for insubordination, desertion or mutiny.

On board the transport ships, wooden sleeping decks were built below deck and across the main deck to stop the convicts coming into contact with the soldiers, crew and free passengers. The barricades separating the convicts from the free passengers had small holes called "loopholes" cut into them so officers could fire their rifles into the convict quarters if the prisoners were trying to mutiny or escape. For every eight men who boarded the transport ships, one died. The death rate for women was lower — one woman died for every 28 women who stepped aboard. Mortality rates on the transport ships were so high that it was eventually decided that ships' surgeons would be paid a bonus for each prisoner who landed safely in New South Wales. Captains who behaved well and treated the convicts humanely were also given a £50 bonus.

A SLOW ROAD TO SUCCESS

Even after the arrival of the Second Fleet, the colony struggled. By November 1791, the weekly rations were cut to just 2.5 pounds of flour and 2 pounds of salted pork each. One of the marines wrote of the convicts lining up for church:

> *They looked the most miserable beings … I ever beheld. They appeared to be worn down with fatigue.*

However, the gardens were finally beginning to grow and Watkin Tench wrote in his journal at the year's end:

> *Vines of every sort seem to flourish: melons, cucumbers, and pumpkins, run with unabounded luxuriancy; and I am convinced that the grapes of New South Wales will, in a few years, equal those of any country.*

The following year, farms began to provide for the colony and Sydney Cove had five stallions and six mares, 43 pigs, 105 sheep, fifteen cows and five calves, as well as chickens, ducks and goats, all of which were used to breed more.

Above: Dairy Cottage, Parramatta park. Dairy farms and gardens at Farm Cove began to help feed the colony about six years after settlement.

Buildings were also beginning to be made more permanent and convicts under the command of the first surveyor-general, Augustus Alt, were employed felling timber to help furnish the colony with more constructions.

Governor Phillip wrote of the colony's difficult early years that many of the problems encountered were just bad luck and "could not have been guarded against, as they never could have been expected". He added, "the Chapter of accidents does not yet open in our favour".

the FACTS!

ON 16 FEBRUARY 1791, *Mary Ann,* the first ship of the Third Fleet, set sail with 150 female convicts on board. Nine died on the ship, which arrived in Sydney on 9 July 1791.

FROM 1 AUGUST to 16 October 1791, the other nine ships of the Third Fleet arrived. Of this contingent, 173 male convicts died on the journey (two of them were executed for attempting mutiny) and nine females died. When the convicts disembarked, as many as 576 were found to be very sick.

THE LAST TRANSPORT of the Third Fleet, the *Queen*, departed from Cork in April 1791. It was the first ship to bring Irish prisoners to New South Wales. Of the 222 male convicts it carried, 172 died less than a year after arriving in Sydney.

MANY OF THE "FREE RANGE" convicts (barracks had not yet been constructed) began to build their own flimsy huts in the area now known as the Rocks.

Above: Fertile land was found at Farm Cove, where Sydney's Botanic Gardens stand today.

Expanding the colony

As well as establishing a settlement, Governor Phillip had also been entrusted with another task, that of exploring and expanding the colony. Little more than a month after his arrival in Port Jackson, he began to seek suitable sites for expansion.

PHILLIP AND HIS OFFICERS first explored Broken Bay and Brisbane Water in a long boat and then rowed west, discovering the mouth of the Hawkesbury River and Pittwater. By April 1788, the governor had ventured as far as Lake Narrabeen and sighted the Blue Mountains, which would later prove such a barrier to further settlement. Moving inland from Sydney Cove, they found suitable land for crops at Farm Cove (Sydney's present-day botanic gardens) and Rose Hill, which was later renamed Parramatta. To the north, Manly Cove was explored and was named after the "confident and manly bearing" of the Aboriginal men Phillip met there.

Above, left to right: Phillip named Manly after the Aborigines he met there; Old Government House at Parramatta was home to ten of the early governors.

NORFOLK ISLAND

As the British Government was concerned that another naval power may attempt to settle Norfolk Island, which Captain Cook had discovered in 1774, Governor Phillip arrived in Botany Bay with the following orders:

Norfolk Island … being represented at a spot which may hereafter become useful, you are, as soon as circumstances will admit of it, to send a small establishment thither to secure the same to us, and prevent it being occupied by the subjects of any other European power.

IN EARLY FEBRUARY 1788, Lieutenant Phillip Gidley King (above left) was dispatched to Norfolk Island in the *Supply* to establish a settlement. He took with him officers, a surgeon, a midshipman and convicts to harvest the natural flax and tall Norfolk Pine. The group settled at Arthurs Vale and began to fell the pine to make buildings. The aim was that Norfolk Island would be self-sufficient and that colonists would grow flax, which was used to make rope and construct boats. Although the tall Norfolk Pines, which had seemed so promising, proved worthless for making ships' masts, the colony continued to grow and by 1792 there were 1115 people on Norfolk. However, the first Norfolk Island settlement was never able to become truly self-sufficient and it was disbanded by 1814.

the FACTS!

NEW SOUTH WALES' second settlement was established at Rose Hill (now Parramatta) on 2 November 1788.

GOVERNOR PHILLIP'S SERVANT Henry Edward Dodd was put in charge of agriculture at Farm Cove, where the Sydney Botanic Gardens stand today. He was renowned for using "infinite tact" to persuade the convicts to work hard at the farm.

MARINES WATKIN TENCH and William Dawes explored the Sydney river system in 1791, discovering that the Hawkesbury and Nepean Rivers were one and the same.

BY 1790, when colonists in Sydney were facing starvation, around one in three convicts was sent to Norfolk Island, where food grew more easily.

BOTH THE SYDNEY and Norfolk (below) penal colonies were to suffer a severe blow when the First Fleet's flagship, the *Sirius*, was wrecked on a coral reef close to the island on 19 March 1790, leaving both colonies isolated.

Above, left to right: Government Offices at Kingston on Norfolk Island; Captain William Paterson.

NORFOLK ISLAND remained uninhabited until June 1825, when a second settlement was established at Kingston. It comprised 57 convicts and a detachment of soldiers under the command of Captain Turton. The penal settlement became infamous as a formidable island prison that housed the worst offenders from New South Wales and Van Diemen's Land. Brutal Lieutenant-Colonel James Morriset was one of the most feared commanders. In 1840, when Captain Alexander Maconochie took over, the colony experienced a couple of years of relative humanity. Maconochie built churches and tried to raise money for books and musical instruments to rehabilitate the convicts, but his ideas were scorned and he was dismissed within two years. The former Hobart Magistrate John Price took over from Maconochie. He was renowned for his viciousness and was eventually bludgeoned to death by convicts at Willimanstown, Victoria, on 26 March 1857. In April of 1852, the Norfolk Island penal settlement was finally closed forever after ongoing reports of inhumane treatment there. Convicts from Norfolk were moved to Van Diemen's Land and the island was occupied by Pitcairn islanders.

IMPENETRABLE MOUNTAINS

Although Watkin Tench and William Dawes first set out from Parramatta to cross the Blue Mountains (right) in 1790, it would be more than two decades before the fertile land of the Bathurst Plains was accessible. Many men failed in their attempts to breach the mountains, which Phillip Gidley King (then Governor of New South Wales) declared "impassable for man" in 1803. Graziers and adventurers Blaxland, Lawson and Wentworth finally crossed the mountains, reaching Katoomba and Mount York on 28 May 1813 to find lush grasslands. Later that year, George Evans pushed further through the mountains, reaching the Macquarie Plains. Within a year, William Cox and a team of convicts had constructed a primitive road through the mountains to Bathurst. Later, in 1815, Evans explored territory around Cowra and discovered the Abercrombie, Belubula and upper Lachlan Rivers. In 1817, Evans accompanied the new surveyor-general, John Oxley, into what would later prove to be some of western New South Wales' most lucrative wool-producing regions.

the FACTS!

NORFOLK ISLAND was called "The Pacific Hell" by convicts.

BY 1792, when Governor Phillip retired, Sydney was making progress. Settlements at Parramatta and Norfolk Island were established and land grants to 70 freed convicts had been made. Subsequent officers Major Francis Grose and William Paterson (above) made more explorations and gave land grants to their fellow soldiers.

FOLLOWING FLINDERS' circumnavigation of the continent in 1803 and the discovery of seals and whales in the south, the colony began to expand to exploit new resources. The English were keen to stop the French, who had been exploring the south, from settling. In September 1803, a group of 49 convicts left Sydney to colonise Van Diemen's Land under the command of 23-year-old Lt John Bowen.

NAVIGATORS and explorers were crucial in opening up pathways for settlement outside of present-day New South Wales. Men such as Hovell and Hume, Louis Barrallier, Mark Currie, John Ovens and ex-convicts Joseph Wild and James Meehan helped put names such as Goulburn, Cooma, Yass and the Monaro Downs on the map.

MAJOR EDMUND LOCKYER, Allan Cunningham and John Oxley moved north, with Cunningham finding the Darling Downs and Oxley and Lockyer exploring the site that became Moreton Bay.

A colony of felons

Some Australians today can trace their lineage to convicts, but not all of the people who came to Australia on the transport ships were "incorrigibles" — some were just unlucky, poverty-stricken children in a time of great deprivation.

THE MAJORITY OF CONVICTS were sentenced for thievery, but some Irish convicts were sentenced for rural crimes. Robbery (known as simple larceny) could receive a sentence of seven years transportation. However, stealing property worth more than a shilling (around $50 today) was known as compound larceny and the sentence was death by hanging. Most of the male convicts had been in trouble with the law before being deported, although many of the female convicts were transported after their first offence.

LOCK OUT THE THIEVES!

With so many thieves and people of loose morals roaming the streets, and no prisons to contain them, it quickly became clear that this colony of felons would need locks to keep convicts out of the stores. One of the convict blacksmiths, a man named Frazer, had been a magician and conjurer before being convicted of theft and receiving stolen goods. When a shipment of locks arrived from England, Frazer simply laughed as he immediately set about picking them with a bent nail!

Above: A convict wearing a yellow and black "magpie suit". *Below right*: Convicts were used to transport goods.

the FACTS!

THE COLONY WAS RIFE with robbery. One prisoner, James Daly, attempted to forge the discovery of gold by grinding down brass shoe buckles and a golden guinea. He was later flogged for his trickery and was eventually hanged for stealing clothing from another convict.

SOME PRISONERS STOLE the Aborigines' tools and sold them to sailors as curios, being paid in rum.

NINE CHILD CONVICTS travelled aboard the First Fleet. They were eleven-year-old James Grace and Sylvester Carthy; John Hudson and John Halfpenny (both aged twelve); Elizabeth Hayward and Mary Branham (both aged thirteen); and John Owen, Charles Kerry and Samuel Peyton (all aged fourteen).

JOHN HUDSON was the youngest convict sentenced to transportation. When he was just eight years old he was sentenced for stealing a linen shirt, one pistol, two aprons and five silk stockings.

ONE OF MARY WADE'S descendants went on to become the Prime Minister of Australia — Kevin Rudd.

FOR THE TERM OF HER NATURAL LIFE

Probably the youngest girl ever transported to Australia was Mary Wade, who was originally sentenced to death at the age of eleven for "assaulting" and "feloniously taking" the clothes of eight-year-old Mary Phillips. Her sentence, unlike that of her fourteen-year-old co-conspirator Jane Whiting, was later changed to transportation "for and during the term of her natural life to the Eastern coast of New South Wales ..." Mary Wade was lucky to survive her journey in the *Lady Juliana* of the Second Fleet and was put ashore at Norfolk Island. She went on to have two children by the age of seventeen and when she died in Sydney, at the grand old age of 82, she had more than 300 descendants!

CONVICT GARB

When the convicts of the First Fleet arrived in Port Jackson, most wore clothes made out of a cheap, flaxen cloth known as osnaburg. However, this rotted very easily and the convicts were soon very ragged. Extra clothes were not carried on the convict ships, so blankets and old clothes were cut up and made into clothing. On 5 July 1788, Governor Philip wrote back to England saying, "a great part of the cloathing [sic] ... was very bad, and a great part of it was likewise too small for people of common size". Governor Macquarie first introduced a striped convict uniform in 1810. The uniforms came in just one size and were marked "PB" for prison barracks. Prisoners at Norfolk Island and Van Diemen's Land wore yellow and black felt uniforms known colloquially as "magpie suits".

Crime & punishment

In the early days of the colony, convicts were quite well treated, provided they steered clear of crime. Later, punishment became more severe. Even minor offences could be punished by stocks, being lashed with the cat-o'-nine tails, treadmill work or death by hanging.

Before arriving in the colony, Governor Phillip believed that only the worst crimes should be punishable by death. He also had bizarre, grisly plans for prisoners who were condemned to death — they would be shipped to New Zealand, where Phillip believed they would be eaten by the Maoris! However, facing starvation in the new colony and unable to control the convicts' compulsive theft, Phillip changed his mind and sentenced anyone caught stealing food to hang. Despite this, other punishments were relatively mild compared to the harsh treatment meted out in later years.

MANGLED AT THE TRIANGLES

The most common punishment was the lash, which the convicts called "being married to the three sisters" (because it had a three-pronged tip) or "being given a present of a red shirt" (a bloody, raw back). In 1834 alone, New South Wales' official register of floggings records that 50,000 lashes were inflicted. Usually, 25 lashes were given for a minor offence and at least 50 for a serious one, which included drunkenness, disobedience, neglect of work, abusive language and disorderly conduct. One farmer who witnessed a flogging at the Bathurst courthouse described the men giving the lash as "bespattered with blood like a couple of butchers". When one of the victims was released, "the blood that had run from his lacerated flesh [squelched] out of his shoes at every step". To make matters worse, a dog was lapping at the blood that ran off the triangles and ants were making off with "great pieces of human flesh" that had been scattered about.

Above: **The Old Mill was built in 1828, on Wickham Terrace, Spring Hill, Brisbane.**

DANCING ACADEMIES

The first convict treadmills (or "dancing academies" as convicts sarcastically called them) were built in 1823 near Carters' Barracks in Sydney and later in Moreton Bay, Port Phillip and Hobart. They consisted of a revolving cylinder attached to a circular iron frame encircled with steps. The drum was filled with stones or attached to a pump or flour mill. Each mill contained up to 36 convicts "treading" for up to fourteen hours, all wearing heavy leg irons. The convicts dreaded the monotony and physical exertion of the treadmills. Anyone who stumbled could be crushed to death and convicts had to grip the hand rail tightly, which led to bleeding, blistered hands. In 1850, 28 convicts at Melbourne's treadmill in Russell Street refused to board the machine, saying they would rather hang.

the FACTS!

THE MILDEST PUNISHMENT was a day in the stocks on the corner of Bathurst and George Streets. The stocks moved to York Street in 1837, close to the market sheds, so passers-by could hurl rotten tomatoes and manure at the felons!

MAGISTRATES could sentence convicts to a chain gang for two years. These "crawlers" worked in irons for up to twelve hours a day. The worst were the lime-burners, who toiled in the lime kilns at Millers Point, Sydney, where the corrosive lime ate into their sensitive flesh.

SOME CONVICTS got full length tattoos of Christ on their backs to signify that the person lashing them was working against Christ's wishes.

EVEN THE LASH couldn't keep some convicts down. Charles Macalister twice saw convicts "deliberately spit, after the punishment, in the flogger's face". Another convict told infamous flogger Black Francis that he "couldn't flog hard enough to kill a butterfly".

REVEREND SAMUEL MARSDEN, the "flogging parson of Parramatta" was one of the most hated disciplinarians. Convicts joked "Lord, have mercy upon us, for His Reverence will have none!"

Uprising & upheaval

Above: John Hunter was the first governor to try to control the activities of the NSW Corps.

Convicts were not the only ones that needed discipline. Members of the New South Wales Corps, who were sent to Sydney to help the governor control convicts, occasionally got out of hand themselves!

the FACTS!

IN MAY 1797, the transport ship the *Lady Shore* was seized by sailors and members of the NSW Corps and sailed to Montevideo, where the Spanish seized it, imprisoned the mutineers and sent the female convicts to work as servants for wealthy Spanish households. Later the same year, in August, prisoners seized the *Cumberland*.

BY 1804, many Irish political prisoners had been transported to Botany Bay. On 4 March, a group of them marched towards Sydney where they planned an uprising at Castle Hill government farm on Sydney's outskirts. Approximately 300 Irish convicts were involved — most of whom had been initially transported for participating in the Irish rebellion of 1798. They recruited a further 1100 convicts and, under the leadership of Philip Cunningham, marched on Parramatta. However, troops had plenty of forewarning and intercepted them at Vinegar Hill, quashing the rebellion and killing some of the men. After the Castle Hill uprising, nine men were hanged and their bodies left to rot in chains as an example. Another 35 rebels were sent to set up a permanent settlement at Coal River, which later became Newcastle.

THE RUM REBELLION

Many officers of the New South Wales Corps made a living out of importing goods and selling them at grossly inflated prices. When the captain of an American ship at port in Sydney refused to sell the marines other provisions unless they purchased the huge supply of rum he had on board, officers of the New South Wales Corps banded together to buy the quantity of spirits. The purchase gave them a monopoly over rum supply in the colony for the next fifteen years and lead to rum becoming a type of currency, encouraging public drunkenness and debauchery.

BY 1795, when Governor John Hunter arrived, the New South Wales Corps virtually owned the colony and some officers, such as John Macarthur, were becoming exceedingly wealthy. Governor Hunter tried to stop officers selling rum at inflated prices, but failed. The next governor, Phillip Gidley King, faced the same problem — an out-of-control New South Wales Corps that had become known as the "Rum Corps". King, too, was unable to stem the colony's trade in liquor.

IN 1805, Governor William Bligh was appointed. Fresh from the mutiny of the *Bounty* and with a reputation for being tough, "Bully Bligh" (as he was known) immediately forbade the use of spirits as trade goods, which upset John Macarthur and other officers and importers. After several attempts to undermine the Bligh administration, Macarthur and six New South Wales Corps officers were arrested by Governor Bligh and charged with treason. However the "Rum Corps" refused to concede to Bligh's rule. Incensed at the treatment of Macarthur (who had become a powerful man), on 26 January 1808, Major Johnston, the commander of the New South Wales Corps, released Bligh's prisoners and arrested the governor instead — an event that became known as the Rum Rebellion.

BLIGH WAS DETAINED for more than a year, then released. He returned to London, where he was vindicated. Major Johnston was later dismissed from the Corps and Macarthur was expelled from the army and fled the colony from 1810–1817 to avoid charges, leaving his estate under the control of his wife Elizabeth.

Right: One of the witnesses of the Rum Rebellion, William Minchin, drew this sketch of Bligh's arrest. Embarrassingly, Governor Bligh hid under the bed when the NSW Corps arrived to overthrow him. The Rum Rebellion ushered in a period of temporary rule in the colony until Lachlan Macquarie took charge in 1810.

Who owns the land?

In 1790, when the colony struggled to survive and provide enough food for its inhabitants, Governor Phillip introduced the first land grants scheme. Since that time, there have been many disagreements over who owns the land and how it should be bought and sold.

UNDER PHILLIP'S COMMAND, convicts who had served their time or been pardoned were granted 30 acres of land. If they were married they received another twenty acres plus an extra ten acres for each child. When soldiers finished their service they were also granted 50 acres and officers who had finished their commission were given 100 acres. It was hoped that ex-convicts, ex-officers and free settlers alike would be able to turn their land into self-sufficient farms, relieving some of the burden on the colony.

THE LAND OWNS US

White settlers were not the only ones claiming a right to land. The Indigenous people of Australia have fought ongoing legal battles to be recognised as the rightful owners of their traditional territory. In 1839, the New South Wales Assistant Protector of Aborigines, William Thomas, wrote about the Aborigines' ideas of land ownership:

> *They hold that the bush and all it contains are man's general property; that private property is only what utensils are carried in the bag; and this general claim to nature's bounty extends even to the successes of the day; hence at the close, those who had been successful divide with those who had not been so. There is no 'complaining in the streets of a native encampment' [begging]; none lacketh while others have it; nor is the gift thought as a favour, but as a right brought to the needy …*

Such a spiritual, egalitarian concept of land ownership gave Aboriginal peoples a disadvantage in white man's law courts until recent Native Title claims were passed.

THE FIRST FARMER

The first ex-convict to be granted land was James Ruse, a Cornishman who had been sentenced to transportation at 22 but had served five years of his seven-year sentence when he was shipped to Australia. As he had a farming background, on 21 November 1789 he was given an acre of cleared land at Parramatta, along with tools, seeds and a small hut, on the condition that he would farm there. He married Elizabeth Parry, another ex-convict, and by 1791 "Experiment Farm" was self-sufficient and the family no longer needed government rations, so the Ruses received a further 29 acres. The farm was constantly raided by convicts. Ruse wrote: "However much I watch my fields, the convicts manage to rob me almost every night".

UNLOCK THE LAND

In 1826, Governor Darling set the "limits of location", which restricted government grants of land to 300 km around the colonies. Settlers ignored these limits and became "squatters" further out. "Unlock the land" soon became the cry from angry people who saw that wealthy squatters controlled large properties on long leases. In 1860, people marched in Melbourne demanding "a vote, a rifle and a farm".

the FACTS!

EXPERIMENT FARM (above) was granted to ex-convict James Ruse in 1789 by Governor Phillip to see "in what time a man might be able to cultivate sufficient quantity of ground to support himself".

ROBERT WEBB and William Reid were also granted land in the early years of the colony, as were eight marines.

BY THE FOURTH YEAR of the colony, 87 people (57 ex-convicts and the rest ex-marines) had been granted land.

ON 21 JUNE 1824, the Australian Agricultural Co was established by a British Act and granted land from Port Stephens to Manning River.

THE LAND GRANTS SYSTEM ended in February 1831, when the British Government instructed Governor Darling to auction all land in New South Wales and Van Diemen's Land at a minimum price of five shillings an acre. In the same year, the Australian Agricultural Co was granted land on the Liverpool Plains, displacing squatters who moved north to settle New England.

Left: Today, Aboriginal park rangers and custodial owners teach others about the Indigenous beliefs associated with the land they have lived on for thousands of years.

A fresh start — pardons & leave

Above: Wealthy merchant Robert Campbell refused to sit on juries with emancipists and called for the cessation of convict transportation in the 1830s.

In 1801, Governor King implemented a "ticket of leave" system that allowed convicts who held a ticket to work for wages, as long as they periodically reported to a magistrate. This operated almost like a good behaviour bond. If convicts on a ticket of leave misbehaved, their ticket would be revoked.

TICKETS OF LEAVE were given to convicts who had behaved well and were able to support themselves. This also meant that they would no longer be a burden on the dwindling Government stores, because they would be able to provide for themselves. Tickets of leave were also issued as a reward for informing on bushrangers or other convicts. Later, Governor Macquarie decided that all convicts had to serve a minimum sentence. Those sentenced to seven year terms could receive a ticket of leave after four years. Those sentenced to fourteen years were eligible after six to eight years of good behaviour. Anybody sentenced to life qualified after ten years. When a prisoner served out their full term (if they had not received a pardon) they were given a Certificate of Freedom.

the FACTS!

IN 1790, Governor Phillip acquired the power to pardon prisoners.

ON 16 DECEMBER 1791, Assistant Surgeon John Irving became the colony's first freed convict.

BY THE 1830s, only about 6% of the convicts were locked up, many others had been pardoned or were working as cheap labour on rural properties.

EVEN WITHIN THE GROUPS there were divisions; some of the well-to-do emancipists wanted nothing to do with recently pardoned convicts. At one dinner, an ex-convict (who had been convicted of another offence in the colony) arrived and would have been thrown out had he not wound the end of the tablecloth tightly around his hand. This was so if he were turned out, all of the food, cutlery and crockery would go with him.

EMANCIPISTS VS EXCLUSIVES

Governor Macquarie believed that convicts who had served their terms or been pardoned should be treated like any other citizen. Freed men became known as "emancipists" and Macquarie urged them to live productive lives. However, many officers and free settlers, known as "exclusives", did not want to associate with ex-convicts. They believed "*Great harm follows from placing the honest man and the thief on equal footing*". Children born in the colony to convict parents were free, but many of the exclusives believed they should be taught in separate schools from their "upper class" children. But Governor Macquarie was adamant that convicts deserved a fair go. The colony was a penal settlement. People who were too proud to mix with convicts should go elsewhere, was Macquarie's opinion.

This division between exclusive and emancipist upset the freed convicts, who felt they had earned the right to a say in how the country was run as much as the free settlers had. In 1821, a group of emancipists sent a petition, signed by 1368 people, to King George IV:

Almost all the people in the colony are convicts or have been convicts. Our labour has cleared the trees, grown the crops, built the towns. We emancipists own more houses and cultivate more land than those who came free. We own more sheep, and shops, and ships. Our total wealth is nearly double those who have never known the feel of a leg iron. We should have the rights of British citizens — a say in how the government is run, and trial by jury. We want to be trusted again, to be given responsible jobs. The land should be ours and our children's! It is our birthright. The colony was founded for convicts.

However, the exclusives were resolute and argued: *Free people — people who have not committed crimes — should have priority over those who have sinned. Why should criminals be rewarded?*

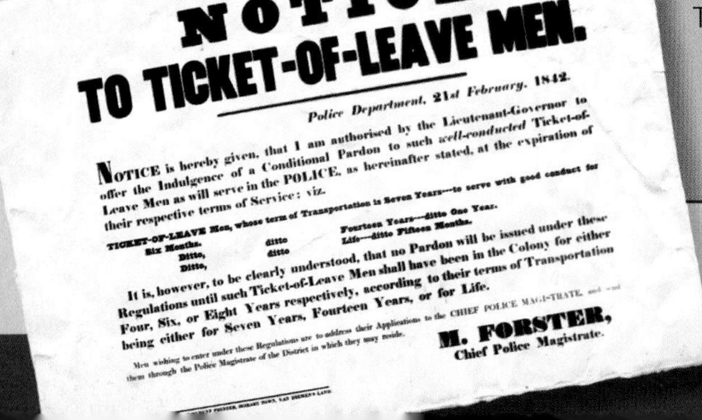

NOTICE
TO TICKET-OF-LEAVE MEN.

Police Department, 21st February, 1842.

NOTICE is hereby given, that I am authorised by the Lieutenant-Governor to offer the Indulgence of a Conditional Pardon to such *well-conducted* Ticket-of-Leave Men as will serve in the POLICE, as hereinafter stated, at the expiration of their respective terms of Service: viz.

TICKET-OF-LEAVE Men, whose term of Transportation is Seven Years—to serve with good conduct for Six Months.
Ditto, ditto Fourteen Years—ditto One Year.
Ditto, ditto Life—ditto Fifteen Months.

It is, however, to be clearly understood, that no Pardon will be issued under these Regulations until such Ticket-of-Leave Men shall have been in the Colony for either Four, Six, or Eight Years respectively, according to their terms of Transportation being either for Seven Years, Fourteen Years, or for Life.

M. FORSTER,
Chief Police Magistrate.

Men wishing to enter under these Regulations are to address their Applications to the CHIEF POLICE MAGISTRATE, and send them through the Police Magistrate of the District in which they may reside.

Left: Notices warned ticket of leave men that they could lose their reprieve for misbehaviour and that turning in bushrangers and other convicts could earn them favours.

The chance of a lifetime

From 1793 to 1830, just 30,000 assisted free settlers came to Australia. However, after 1830 the number of migrants swelled. By 1840, more settlers than convicts were being shipped to Australia, with 65,000 free settlers between 1831–40 compared to 51,000 convicts.

A DIFFICULT, DANGEROUS VOYAGE

By the 1850s, life on the settler ships was often harsher than on the convict transports, and the berth size and rations for a third-class migrant and a convict were about the same. In 1883, Dr Scott Skirving, travelling aboard the *Ellora* wrote: *"It was horrid and even indecent for decent married people to be herded together like beasts, with almost no privacy [to] dress or undress ..."* It took 100–120 days to sail to New South Wales from England and the barque-rigged ships free settlers sailed on were slow (around 9 km/h) and rollicking. Poorer settlers occupied the steerage or third-class section below deck, where they were crammed into narrow berths separated from others by a curtain. Steerage passengers slept, prepared food and ate in this section, which often stank and was very unhygienic. Wealthier travellers in first and second class had cabins with bunks, cupboards, hand basins and a chamber pot.

HUTS WITH DIRT FLOORS

Settlers were told to take an astonishing list of items with them because very little could be bought in the colony. Among other things, they needed six axes, one tonne of flour, two chests of tea, twelve pocket knives, twelve blankets, three cross-cut saws and 100 pounds of nails, as well as six hoes, six spades and a plough. This made travelling to their plot cumbersome. Once settlers arrived, most set up tents and began clearing land to build a slab hut. The floor was usually mud, dirt, or clay from a termite's nest stamped down firmly; sometimes boards were laid on the floor. Settler Emma Loader reminisced about settling on the Coolgardie goldfields in 1896: *The first thing ... was to cut some posts and dig holes and put them in the ground, then cut corn sacks open and sew them together and nail them to the posts, then I put the iron on it for a roof and sewed more bags up and lined it inside too ... I papered the inside with newspapers and whitewashed the outside, it was quite a smart house..."* Extreme drought, bushfire and the risk of attack by Aborigines were just some of the trials settlers faced. They also struggled to understand the seasons and plant enough food to support themselves.

Above: Detail from James Fagan's artwork *The Emigrant's Farewell*. Many emigrants never returned to visit friends and family in England.

the FACTS!

ON 16 FEBRUARY 1793, the colony's first free settlers arrived on the *Bellona* — they consisted of just nine people including four children and made their home at Liberty Plains (today's Bankstown). They were Thomas Rose with his wife and four children, Thomas and Joseph Web and Frederick Meredith.

THERE WAS NO CUTLERY, crockery or tables and chairs on immigrant ships, so migrants had to bring their own. Meals were small and many people starved to death. Ellen Moger, who travelled from England to South Australia in 1840, lost three of her four children to starvation on the voyage.

SHIPWRECK was a frightening possibility and ships such as the *Loch Ard* and the *Cataraqui* sank, claiming many lives.

Left, top to bottom: A settler's hut preserved at Rockhampton Historical Museum; Convicts called the new settlers "New chums" or "Jimmy Grants". They made fun of the way they dressed and their limited knowledge about the continent.

Above: Former actor and pickpocket George Barrington redeemed himself in Sydney.

Fame & fortune

Some of the settlers became extremely wealthy in their new country, but even more surprising was that many convicts rose to fame and fortune from the depths of despair.

the FACTS!

ON 15 SEPTEMBER 1790, Britain's Old Bailey sentenced actor George Barrington to seven years transportation for pickpocketing. Barrington was known for his eloquence and had talked his way out of his crimes several times. In New South Wales, he was granted emancipation for good behaviour and became the superintendent of convicts at Parramatta.

PRETTY ESTHER ABRAHAMS was just seventeen when she was sentenced to seven years transportation for stealing a piece of black lace from the millinery shop in which she worked. However, on board the First Fleet she soon caught the eye of Lieutenant George Johnston of the marines and, upon arriving in Sydney, moved in with him as his de facto wife. Later, George was promoted to major and, after deposing and arresting Governor Bligh in 1808, acted as the provisional governor for nearly six months. Despite having a family and land together, Esther and Major Johnston were only married in 1814, after fourteen years together.

Below: Macquarie Lighthouse, a replica of the original designed by Greenway.

LORDING IT OVER THEM

Simeon Lord (below left) was sentenced to seven years transportation to New South Wales in 1791 and became one of Australia's earliest entrepreneurs. After finishing his sentence in 1798, he traded as a merchant before becoming the public auctioneer in 1801. He expanded his business portfolio to a tanning works in the early 1800s and then a textile mill in 1815. Governor Macquarie later appointed Simeon Lord as a magistrate.

CAPABLE KABLE

Henry Kable and Susannah Holmes were both transported to New South Wales for fourteen years for break and enter. They were among the five couples married by Revered Richard Johnson after the First Fleet landed. Henry Kable soon impressed Governor Phillip and was given the job of supervising other convicts, later being made the chief constable (until he was sacked for selling rum to convicts!). However, by the early 1800s, after serving his sentence, he set up a whaling and sealing company and became very wealthy, exporting his wares around the world.

A CONVICT ARCHITECT

Francis Greenway was an English architect who arrived in Sydney in 1814 after being sentenced to transportation for forgery. When he arrived in the colony, he carried with him a reference from former governor John Hunter to Governor Lachlan Macquarie, recommending Greenway's skills. His background was extremely useful in the colony, so he was granted a ticket of leave and began designing buildings by 1815.

HE DESIGNED AND SUPERVISED the construction of around 40 buildings, including St Matthew's Church and the Court House at Windsor, the lighthouse at South Head and St James Church in Sydney, as well as stables for Government House (which is now the New South Wales Conservatorium of Music). Greenway received a complete pardon in 1819, but was dismissed as the assistant engineer to the colony in 1822 when he demanded an architect's fee on top of his government salary. He continued in private practice, but, unfortunately, many people considered him hot-tempered and pompous and he made many enemies by criticising other Sydney buildings and architectural works. Few builders wanted to work with Greenway and he died a poor man in 1837.

WEALTH FROM PENURY

Thomas Reibey, the former first mate of a Dutch East India trading ship, left his ship in 1793 to settle in Sydney. Years earlier, Lancashire-born Mary Haydock had been transported to New South Wales for stealing a horse. (At the time of her sentencing she had been dressed as a boy and it was only discovered that she was a thirteen-year-old girl after she was sentenced.) Little did the thirteen-year-old know she would end up being one of the fledgling colony's wealthiest matriarchs.

MARY ARRIVED IN SYDNEY in 1792 and worked for Major Francis Grose before marrying Thomas Reibey. The couple were given a grant of land in the Hawkesbury River region and established a farm; however, Thomas also set up a timber and grain shipping business, which soon extended to trading in seal skins. Mary Reibey managed the farms while Thomas was away and then moved to Sydney in 1806 and opened a store. After her husband died of a fever in 1811, Mary continued to manage the family's farms and businesses herself, becoming the colony's richest woman. She also financed the construction of several substantial buildings in Macquarie Place and was involved with a number of charities.

FELON TO SURGEON

Australia's first teacher of medical students, William Redfern, was convicted of leading an attempted mutiny in the British Navy and sentenced to transportation to New South Wales in 1801. By 1802, he was appointed assistant surgeon for Norfolk Island and was pardoned in 1803. He continued to work at Norfolk for a further five years before returning to Sydney, where he worked as the assistant surgeon for the colony until 1819. He later served at Dawes Point hospital and established the most renowned private practice in New South Wales. Governor Lachlan Macquarie appointed Redfern as a magistrate in 1819, but this was over-ruled by commissioner Bigge because of Redfern's convict past. Redfern was one of the foremost emancipists, who believed that ex-convicts had the right to be treated as equals. In 1821, he led a delegation to England that resulted in laws that limited opportunities for ex-convicts to be repealed in the British courts. The Sydney suburb of Redfern is named after this famous ex-convict.

HIGHWAYMAN TO CHIEF POLICE MAGISTRATE

D'Arcy Wentworth was born in Ireland and studied as a doctor in London, where he was twice charged (but acquitted) with highway robbery. He travelled aboard the Second Fleet in 1789 as assistant surgeon and was sent to be superintendent of convicts on Norfolk Island in 1791. In 1809, he was promoted to principal surgeon of the civil medical department at Parramatta, which he held until he retired. Governor Macquarie appointed D'Arcy Wentworth chief police magistrate, superintendent of police and honorary treasurer of the police fund and he became a founder-director of the Bank of New South Wales in 1816. He was also a major contractor of Sydney's Rum Hospital. D'Arcy's son William, along with Gregory Blaxland and William Lawson, crossed the Blue Mountains in 1813.

the FACTS!

JOHN PASCOE FAWKNER (above), founder of Melbourne, came to Australia with his convict father in 1803 and was frequently in trouble with the law. For helping some convicts escape in 1814, he received 500 lashes and three years hard labour. Later, he opened a hotel in Launceston and by 1828 had established himself as the editor of the *Launceston Advertiser*. After landing in Port Phillip in 1835, he ran a hotel and began the first newspaper in Port Phillip, the *Melbourne Advertiser*, which was at first shut down because he had not bothered to obtain the proper licence to print a newspaper. He went on to run the *Port Phillip Patriot* and *Melbourne Advertiser*. Despite being declared bankrupt in 1845, Fawkner was still elected to the first Legislative Council in 1851!

ANDREW BENT was an English convict who arrived in Hobart in 1812 and later championed freedom of the press in Tasmania. He soon became the government printer and printed the first *Hobart Town Gazette* and *Southern Reporter* in 1816. Bent opposed the colonial administration at the time, and often published inflammatory articles, which saw him fined and imprisoned by Governor Arthur. In 1839, he moved to Sydney and published *Bent's News* and *New South Wales Publisher*. Unfortunately, while Bent found fame, fortune eluded him and he died penniless in 1851.

Making a living in a new land

Europeans struggled to make a living out of the new land at first, but soon ushered in two centuries of prosperity that relied on agriculture, farming introduced domestic species, or digging up, chopping down and exporting Australia's wealth of natural resources.

Above: Shearing employed many men and boys, who at first used hand shears until electric shears were introduced.

the FACTS!

CONVICT ELIJAH LEEKS started Australia's first manufacturing industry in 1788 when he used local clay to start a pottery at Wentworth Avenue, Sydney.

SOME FAMILIES, such as the Hentys and the Imlay brothers based near Eden, NSW, harvested whales during the whaling season and grazed cattle at other times.

BY 1802, more than 25,000 seal skins were being exported. By the 1830s, seal populations had declined so much that the industry was no longer viable.

IN 1847, Henry and William Dangar opened the first beef canning factory at Newcastle, NSW.

A GUN SHEARER named Jacky Howe managed to shear 321 sheep in just seven hours and 40 minutes, using a hand shear, in 1892.

IN 1901, WILLIAM FARRER experimented with wheat breeds to create a fast-growing, rust-resistant strain called Federation wheat.

TIMBER-GETTING quickly became a prosperous occupation, especially in north Queensland and in New South Wales' "Big Scrub".

BLOOD MONEY

Whaling (above) was one of Australia's first and most lucrative primary industries, beginning in 1788. Within 50 years, whaling stations had been established along the east coast from Moreton Bay to Hobart. At the time, seal and whale oil were used to fuel lights and used in the production of margarine, soap and perfume. Underneath their bodices, ladies wore tight corsets that had whalebone and baleen sewn into them. The pelts of seals were also highly sought after and were traded in China for goods such as silk and tea. Seal skins were also used to make capes, gloves and other clothing. When the *Sydney Cove* ran aground on Preservation Island in the Bass Strait in 1797, sailors reported that seals were abundant on the island and sealers were quick to capitalise. Within years, seal populations were decimated.

GRAINS OF GOLD

Wheat was first planted at Farm Cove and farmed by James Ruse, but was not grown in large quantities until it was planted around Bathurst in 1816 — the region quickly became the colony's main source of wheat. When South Australian settler John Ridley invented a wheat harvester in 1843, the wheat industry was able to rapidly expand. Prior to this, a lack of labour meant it took much longer to harvest wheat. In 1883, Australian wheat was first exported to England and during the 19th century wheat farms were established in all the Australian colonies. The Australian wheat industry is now worth more than eight billion dollars annually, even though it comprises just 3% of Australia's exports.

Above, left to right: **The nation remains one of the world's largest wool producers; Australia now has many successful vineyards and exports more wine to the United Kingdom than France does.**

ON THE SHEEP'S BACK

Some historians consider that Australia rode to prosperity on the sheep's back. Certainly by 1830, wool production had taken over from sealing and whaling as the colony's main source of income. By 1849, more than sixteen million sheep grazed these shores. The lack of refrigeration made meat export difficult, so mutton was considered less important than wool production until 1879, when refrigerated meat was able to be shipped from Sydney.

AN AUSTRALIAN TIPPLE

The first grape vines were planted at Farm Cove in 1788, but it was not until 1822 that Gregory Blaxland sent the first shipment of Australian wine to London. The following year, Blaxland's wine won a silver medal in a British Wine show and the Australian wine industry was assured.

In 1824, James Busby planted vine cuttings from Spanish and French grapes at Farm Cove and in the Hunter Valley in New South Wales. Cuttings were also planted in Victoria in 1838 and in South Australia by 1839. However, wool industry pioneers John and Elizabeth Macarthur became the continent's first large viticultural suppliers when, in 1827, their vineyard produced 90,000 L of wine. German immigrants, most fleeing religious persecution, initiated the lucrative Barossa Valley wine industry in the 1840s. Thomas Hardy also went on to be a major player in the viticulture industry.

the **FACTS!**

BY 1830, Australia was exporting about 900,000 kg of wool annually. Within ten years, this amount increased to 3.5 million kg and then to 17.5 million kg by 1850.

FARMERS near Port Macquarie in New South Wales tried growing a crop of sugar cane in 1822, but found the climate unsuitable. By 1847, cane farmers in Queensland (below) found that the crop was well suited to the humid climate. West Indian born John Buhot produced the first granulated sugar in Queensland in 1862 and received a land grant of just over 200 ha to expand the sugar cane industry. He then helped Captain Louis Hope to plant around 8 ha under cane near Ormiston, Queensland. Hope went on to build Australia's first commercial sugar mill.

GRAZIERS & MILKERS

Dairy cattle arrived on the First Fleet and the diary industry was first established at Parramatta. However, by about 1820, the Illawarra District of New South Wales had become the hub for dairy products. Cheese and butter from the region was carted to Sydney on packhorses or shipped on boats.

The beef industry had a slow start because refrigerated ships only made exporting frozen beef possible in the 1880s.

Above: **Dairy farming was the salvation of many small landholders, particularly in the Illawarra district where farmers survived by selling butter, cheese and milk.**

KEEPING STORE

Farming was not the only way to make money in the new colonies. Many enterprising businessmen set up shop and profited from the lack of competition in isolated areas. Storekeepers could often charge whatever they liked because they knew it would still be cheaper and easier than travelling to the city to buy goods. At first, these frontier store owners made a lot of money, but with time transport improved and more shops were opened to provide competition, so prices were lowered.

Above: Some Aborigines, such as Bennelong, became distanced from their culture because of their relationship with Europeans.

Assistance, resistance & reprisal

At first, the Aboriginal people were curious about the strange white men and women, and some even helped them out. However, after a while, once they realised these "visitors" were here to take over their traditional lands, naturally Aborigines tried to resist the invasion.

SOME TOOK to attacking convicts and settlers and spearing livestock, sparking bloody confrontations. Both Aborigines and white settlers were killed in the years of conflict that followed, but many more Aborigines than Europeans lost their lives. Aboriginal culture and beliefs were difficult for the settlers to fathom. They could not understand why the Aborigines did not want to wear clothes or live in houses. The Aborigines, conversely, could not understand why the white people should require such things. Despite the conflict, some Aborigines and Europeans formed firm friendships and many Aborigines provided invaluable help to the settlers. Often they worked as trackers and guides for explorers; as native police; on farms or as station hands mustering cattle; or working as cooks or domestic servants.

Above: Settlers and Aborigines often came into conflict, although some governors tried hard to provide justice for both parties.

the FACTS!

GOVERNOR PHILLIP believed in the concept of the "noble savage" popularised by philosopher Jean-Jacques Rousseau — that "natives" were naturally more honest and noble than greedy Europeans. He wrote, "*I shall think it a great point gained if I can proceed … without having any great dispute with the natives; a few of them I shall … settle near us … to furnish* [them] *with everything that can tend to civilise them, and give them a high opinion of their new guests*".

MOST EUROPEANS couldn't understand the Aboriginal way of life. They hoped to bring Christianity to Aborigines and believed that children who were given a Christian education would be integrated into white society, so they forcibly removed Aboriginal children from their families.

SOME ABORIGINES requested that the white men use their guns against tribal enemies and were upset when they would not. But the Aborigines hated the hangings and floggings they saw meted out by the white men on the convicts.

BRAVE PEMULWUY of the Dharug people gathered a force of 100 warriors and fought a twelve-year battle of resistance with European settlers, making raids at Toongabbie and Parramatta in 1797 and torching farms around the colony.

A FISH OUT OF WATER

Bennelong ("great fish") was a tall warrior of the Wanghal tribe who could spear up to twenty fish in an afternoon. In 1789, he and his friend Colbee were caught by Captain Phillip, who wanted to know how to find native food. Colbee escaped, but Bennelong did not seem to mind living in the colony, so his leg-irons were removed. He learned English quickly and called Governor Phillip *Be-anna* — the name given to the most respected elder. In return, Phillip called Bennelong *Dooroow*, which means son. Bennelong later accompanied Phillip to England, where he learnt to skate, box and even met King George III. On his return, he urged his people to adopt the English way of life. Bennelong's sister ran from Botany Bay to greet him, but he was angry that she was not clothed. The Wanghal people were wary of this new, anglicised Bennelong. He gave one of his wives a bonnet and petticoat as a gift, so she left him. Other women refused his advances and he lost the respect of his tribe. He lived a lonely life in his brick house and later lost the respect of the colonists when he turned to alcohol. Bennelong died an outcast in 1813. Bennelong Point, where the Opera House stands, is named after this friendly Aborigine.

TRUGANINI OF TASMANIA

Brave, proud Truganini (left) was born on Bruny Island, off the Tasmanian coast, and is remembered for her efforts to save Tasmanian Aborigines from attack by white settlers. Settlers killed her sister, mother and the man she was to marry and abducted and raped Truganini when she was just a young woman. Later, Governor Arthur persuaded her to help George Robinson resettle Aborigines on Flinders Island off the north-east coast of Tasmania. Truganini later told historian James Calder, "I knew it was no use my people trying to kill all the white people now; there were so many of them always coming in big boats". Unfortunately, the Aborigines did not find peace on Flinders Island, where housing was poor, they were badly treated and Robinson tried to convert them to Christianity. By 1873, all apart from Truganini had died from disease and deprivation. In 1876, Truganini, regarded as the last full-blood member of her tribe, died in Hobart.

Above: **William Barak, an inspirational leader and protester against the removal of Aboriginal reserves.**

WINDRADYNE THE WARRIOR

When settlers began to encroach on the land of the Wiradjuri people of New South Wales in the 1820s, fierce Windradyne was determined to stop them. In 1822, Windradyne and his tribesmen attacked outlying stations and led raids to set fire to buildings, attack garrisons and kill sheep and cattle in retaliation for violent acts against his people. Governor Thomas Brisbane was so worried by the men's resistance that he declared martial law. After a raid on a property near Bathurst, Windradyne was captured and detained by six soldiers. He spent a month in chains before being released with a strong warning. Troops later invaded his homeland and one-third of the Aboriginal population was massacred. To make peace, Windradyne and 400 members of his tribe walked 200 km to Parramatta to meet Governor Brisbane. In a letter published in *The Australian* on 4 October 1826, Windradyne is described as "*... without doubt, the most manly black native we have ever beheld ... he is supposed to have suffered severely*".

THE BATTLE OF PINJARRA

Aborigines resisted the invasion of tribal lands around Swan River in 1829, but when they killed a trooper named Hugh Nesbit in 1834 it sparked a bloody reprisal. In what became known as the Battle of Pinjarra, or the Pinjarra massacre, Governor Stirling and his soldiers surrounded a group of Aborigines near the Murray River south of Perth. After spears were thrown, up to 30 of the Aborigines were shot dead. Two settlers were wounded in the melee, after which the Aborigines abandoned their traditional land in fear.

BRAVE BARAK

People of the Woiwurrong tribe of Victoria's grasslands were moved to Aboriginal reserves when pastoralists began to take their land. In the 1860s, Barak and another man, Wonga, led their people to the Coranderrk reserve. When the Board for the Protection of Aborigines proposed to take the land in 1865, Barak negotiated with the government and campaigned for support among Victorian high society. Barak and his people won and the BPA gave up trying to disband Coranderrk in 1886. The reserve was later closed in 1924.

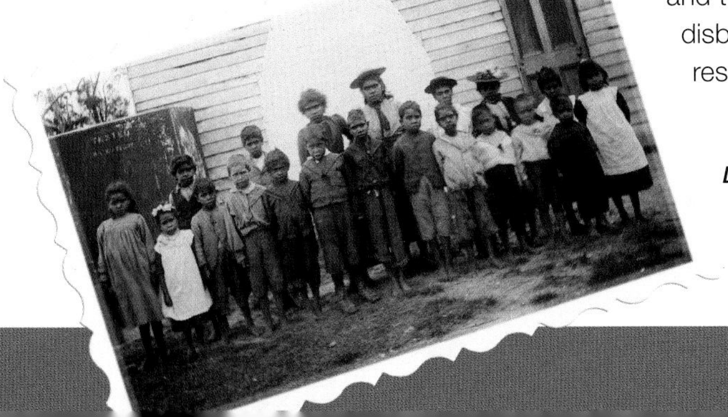

Left: **Aboriginal children were often removed from their families and sent to State homes or schools.**

the FACTS!

MYALL CREEK STATION became the site of one of Australia's most infamous massacres when, in 1838, eleven convict stationhands, under the command of the squatter's son, rounded up and murdered thirty Aboriginal men, women and children in retaliation for an attack on some shepherds. The men were arrested and tried for murder, but were found not guilty. However, Governor Gipps, on hearing that Aboriginal children had been among the victims, had them retried and seven of the men were hanged.

SOME TERRIBLE ACTS were committed on both sides, but far more Aborigines were killed than white settlers. An estimated 10,000 Aborigines occupied Victoria. In fifteen years, 59 white people were killed by Aborigines while at least 400 Aborigines were killed. Many Europeans believed the Aborigines would soon die out and some of the Aborigines even spoke sadly of their own doom. "Black man die fast since white man came," one said, "Soon no blackmen, all whitemen."

SETTLERS AND ABORIGINES came into conflict often in Tasmania, where Aborigines fiercely resisted European takeover and attacks by settlers. In October 1830, settlers tried to drive out the Aborigines; six men formed a line and walked across the country, chasing Aborigines with dogs. However, the Aborigines were masters of surviving in the bush and only one Aboriginal man and boy were caught.

Above: Squatters dwelt in slab huts until they could afford to build more luxurious homes.

Squatting for a living

In the early days of settlement, the British Government tried to limit expansion of the colonies to around 300 km from the nineteen known counties of New South Wales. However, graziers seeking their fortune often ignored this and established large grazing properties beyond the zone and in rich farmlands elsewhere. They became known as squatters and many of them made a lucrative living off the land.

MOST OF THE LANDHOLDERS closer to the colony were ex-convicts and graziers on land grants, who sold their cattle to markets in Sydney. Larger properties further out were squats on illegally obtained land controlled by wealthy exclusives, many of whom later left the run to live a refined life in the cities, leaving the properties under the control of shepherds.

NOT FOR THE FAINT-HEARTED

Squatting was not an easy existence in the early days of establishing a run. After finding suitable land, squatters such as the Henty brothers had to drove livestock long distances to the runs they had found. Once there, they lived in tents while they constructed rickety huts made of roughly hewn timber and stringybark bound together with rawhide, because nails were expensive. Sometimes wattle-and-daub huts were built by shaping moist mud over a framework of wattle twigs and then leaving it to dry. Hardwood shutters affixed to leather hinges kept snakes and possums out of the homestead. Chimneys were smoky, ineffectual affairs, made of slate or hardwood slabs lined inside with flattened-out tins. Timber packing cases and kerosene tins were converted to furniture and cupboards, and beds usually consisted of little more than sheepskins strung between springy saplings, or a flattened bark slab raised up by two parallel logs. There was no bathroom and the toilet was a "long drop" (a deep hole with a small hut built over it and a tin can for a toilet seat). At night, the only light came from a burning candle wick placed in solidified mutton fat.

Above: The Squatter's First Home, depicted by Alexander Denistoun Lang.

the FACTS!

SQUATTING WAS ILLEGAL until Governor Bourke legalised it in 1836 by insisting that squatters lease the land at a cost of £10 a year.

WHEN SQUATTERS first arrived at their "squat" they burnt a line of trees on each horizon to act as a boundary for their run.

A SHEPHERD'S LIFE was considered an ideal way to reform convicts because shepherds lived far away from others, where they could get up to little mischief.

FLOUR, SUGAR, TEA and golden syrup were essential parts of a squatter's diet. Damper cooked in the ashes of the fire was a staple, and mutton was often eaten up to three times a day. The poor diet often resulted in a skin condition known as "Barcoo rot".

SQUATTERS AND SETTLERS tied a piece of twine, known as a "bowyang", around the bottom of each trouser leg to help keep out snakes and dirt. Hats made of woven together cabbage-tree palm protected them from the sun.

MEN SQUATTED ALONE at first, then, once they had some wealth behind them, went to town to seek wives. The *Old Bullock Dray* ballad jokes that ladies loved a squatter: *Oh! the shearing is all over, and the wool is coming down/And I mean to get a wife, boys, when I go down to town/Everything's that's got two legs presents itself to view/From the little paddy-melon [sic] to the bucking kangaroo.*

Above, left to right: Inside an early squatter's homestead preserved at the Rockhampton Historical Museum; The squatter's dining room; When squatters grew richer, they built grand Victorian houses.

THE LANDED GENTRY

Squatters soon grew wealthy from the sale of wool and began to employ others to care for their properties and their stock. Often several large flocks of sheep were herded across vast properties, so squatters required many stockmen and shepherds. Convict shepherds drove the sheep by day and penned them by night to protect them from Dingoes and Aborigines. As well as having to clear land for grazing, squatters also had to transport wool and meat to market, so they seasonally had to employ timber-getters, shearers and bullock drivers. By the 1840s, many squatters had an enviable lifestyle, employing migrants and settlers as servants, butchers, tanners and shearers. As the squatters' fortunes grew, they began to upgrade to large colonial homesteads, often with wide verandahs, timber floors and glazed windows. The kitchen was usually outside the house to reduce the risk of fire and keep smoke out of the living areas. Often the squatter's original shanty huts were converted into the servants' quarters or kitchen. Despite becoming some of Australia's wealthiest families, most of the squatters had built their empires through hard work, rather than inheritance. They were able to equal their employees in knowledge, determination and grit, and, as such, squatters were initially well-respected, unlike the English upper-class landed gentry.

Above: A cartoon entitled *Back Country Squatter AD 1892* shows a squatter on the road to ruin. Not only is he wading through debt, but he is laden down with problems such as locust and rabbit plagues, stock taxes, drought and a hefty mortgage.

THE END OF SQUATTING

By the 1870s, squatters dominated land ownership and ex-convicts and settlers began to complain; they wanted to own farms too, but the squatters were monopolising the land. To counter the problem, the government made squatters lease their runs and then opened up land for selection. Most squatters made a lot of money until the economic depression of the 1890s, when the price of wool dropped dramatically. During this time, millions of sheep and cattle were boiled down to tallow (a type of fat used to make candles and soap), which was at the time worth more than wool. Some squatters went heavily into debt to buy their runs once land was available for selection; others had chosen a "back country" run in a good season, not realising that the area usually experienced crippling drought. Rabbit plagues and high-interest mortgages added to their woes and forced some squatters off the land.

the FACTS!

AS THE AFFLUENT SQUATTERS began to put on airs and graces, their staff began to stop respecting them and a "class war" widened the gap between the rich and the poor. A ballad named *The Sheepwasher's Lament* complains: *When I first went a-washing sheep/The year was sixty-one/The master was a worker then/ The servant was a man/But now the squatters, puffed with pride/ They treat us with disdain/Lament the days that are gone by/Ne'er to return again.*

RICH SQUATTER Charles Ebden of Carlsruhe, Victoria, was nicknamed "the Count" because he had a separate "traveller's cottage" for guests and refused to talk to any but the most important visitors.

SQUATTERS TRIED to outdo each other with Italianate mansions. Thomas Chirnside's Werribee Park Mansion took five years to build and cost a fortune. Less than ten years after it was completed, Chirnside, believing himself bankrupt, committed suicide.

MANY SQUATTERS were Scottish so it was commonly said that "the Scotch [sic] own the land and the Irish own the pubs".

Justice served
— establishing law & order

The biggest problem in the colony's early years was that the convicts could not be contained. There were no gaols, and although the dense bush and threat of death stopped many escapees from "bolting", there was no real way to isolate the extreme villains from the general crooks.

Above: David Collins, the first judge-advocate, went on to found a settlement at Van Diemen's Land.

CONSEQUENTLY, storerooms had barred windows to keep the convicts out, but the convicts roamed around at will. There was no secure imprisonment because to begin with, there were simply no buildings to imprison them in! Even the huts and outbuildings constructed in the early days were not secure enough to contain hardened criminals. Only later did Governor Macquarie build barracks to contain convicts and real gaols were later constructed at Norfolk Island, Port Arthur and Moreton Bay. These gaols all contained felons who had committed crimes on Australian soil, not those transported from England.

UNWILLING JURORS

Initially, the Sydney penal colony was run like a military establishment. Governor Phillip had the power to appoint constables and justices, grant reprieves and pardons, raise armed forces, construct fortifications, grant land and control the colony's financial affairs. Criminal charges were dealt with under the *Mutiny Act* and the Articles of War. A Provost arranged for sentences to be conducted and the available punishments were flogging or death.

Captain David Collins, a marine who had no former legal experience, was appointed Sydney's first judge-advocate — a difficult task that required him to chair the tribunal, which worked as a criminal court and included the judge-advocate and six naval or military officers. He also had to advise on points of British law and act as a prosecutor. However, many of the marines did not want to sit as members of the criminal court because they were not paid any extra to do so. The marines, all of whom were volunteers when they set out from England, began to suffer from associating with convicts. They consumed much rum and were even accused of stealing supplies on occasion.

PROBLEMATIC POLICEMEN

Policing the new colony presented real problems. Even London had no police force until 1829, so finding a force to control convicts was a challenge. The marines, under the command of cantankerous Major Robert Ross, insisted they were sent to Sydney as soldiers, not to be policemen or gaolers; they refused to help control the convicts, leaving Phillip little choice but to establish a convict guard. By August 1789, because of the lack of law and order and the scarce rations, thefts were occurring almost every night, both from stores and from private farms. The first Australian police force, comprised of convicts, was therefore formed and called the "Night Watch".

Right: Norfolk Island evening re-enactment.

the FACTS!

JUDGE-ADVOCATE David Collins handed down sentences in the first criminal court, which was established shortly after settlement. Regular punishments were lashings and a convict might receive 25 strokes for stealing or as many as 150 for assaulting a marine.

THE FIRST MAN to be tried was Samuel Barsby, who was sentenced to 150 lashes for assaulting a marine. Another convict, James Tennihill, who stole bread, was imprisoned on Pinchgut Island and given nothing but bread and water to eat for a week.

JOHN HARRIS, the first chief of the convict police force, had been sentenced to transportation for stealing eight silver teaspoons.

THE FIRST MEMBERS of the newly appointed New South Wales Corps arrived with the Second Fleet in 1790 to replace the unwilling marines that had come out on the First Fleet. Their duty was to obey the Governor's commands, guard the convicts and act as judges for the criminal court. Many members of the Corps felt that they had the opportunity to make their fortune in the new colony.

GOVERNOR MACQUARIE was the first soldier to govern the colony, all others were naval officers.

A NATIVE Police Force began in Victoria in 1837, and again in 1842.

Left: A cell inside old Melbourne Gaol.

Above: The Old Courthouse and Police Station at Willunga, South Australia, was established in 1855.

Above, right: The most incorrigible convicts to have committed crimes on Australian soil were kept behind bars at the penitentiary, Port Arthur, Tasmania.

Judge-Advocate David Collins wrote: *It was to have wished, that a watch established for the preservation of public and private property had been formed of free people … But there was not any choice. The military had their line of duty marked out for them, and between them and the convict there was no description of people from whom overseers or watchman could be provided.*

Instead, a Jewish convict named John Harris became the colony's first chief of police. This made life for the convicts much easier than it would have been had the marines been the police force. At night, there was a curfew after a "taptoo" drum had been beat. The colony was split into sections, each under the command of a night-watchman who was to "inform himself of the actual residence of each individual in his district, as well as of his business, connections, acquaintance" … and to be aware of "such convicts as may sell or barter their slops [clothes] or provisions, as also of such as game for either of the aforesaid articles [gambling their clothes]" … to report any robberies and detail any "soldiers or seaman found straggling after the taptoo has beat, or who may be found in the convicts' huts".

The new guard offended Major Ross and the other marines, who thought it unseemly that a convict night-watchman was able to arrest drunken soldiers! The night-watchmen were not popular with the convicts either and Collins' diary notes read they were "held in fear and detestation" by their fellow man. However, they were effective and by November 1789, crimes had decreased considerably.

the FACTS!

CONVICT JF Mortlock recorded how the convicts saw the guards: *"Men betraying their companions or accepting authority over them, are often called 'dogs', and sometimes have their noses bitten off — the morsel being termed 'a mouthful of a dog's nose'".*

IN 1823, THE LEGISLATIVE Council and Supreme Court were established under the *New South Wales Act 1823 (UK).*

CONSTITUTIONAL independence was first given to Tasmania in 1825 and the legislative bodies were nominated until Tasmania gained its first partly elected council in 1850.

WESTERN AUSTRALIA was granted responsible elected government in 1890.

IN 1852, the *Constitution Act* established a partially elected legislative council in South Australia. A similar political landscape existed in Queensland, which was part of New South Wales until 1859, when it was granted self-government under Sir George Bowen.

ELECTED REPRESENTATION

From 1788 to 1821, each of the colonies was controlled by a governor who made decisions about the colony in conjunction with the British sovereign and British parliamentary Acts. The governors did not make the laws, but they did try to adapt English law to suit life in the colonies. Gradually, the political system in the colonies moved towards representative government, with the *New South Wales Judicature Act (1823)* creating legislative councils that advised the governor on political issues. A new, mostly elected legislative council was formed in 1842 and in 1850 the *Australian Colonies Government Act* allowed for the establishment of a common form of government for the eastern colonies. This included councils with elected members, which could amend the constitution.

Right: **This cartoon entitled *The First Parliament of Botany Bay in High Debate* makes fun of the general lawlessness of the colony's early days.**

Above: Lieutenant-Governor Francis Grose of the NSW Corps.

The colony of New South Wales

After Governor Phillip, who had fallen ill, had retired to England in December 1791, the colony passed into the hands of a succession of New South Wales Corps rulers until Governor John Hunter began a five-year term in 1795.

A "GROSE" ABUSE OF POWER

Phillip's choice for successor had been Phillip Gidley King, who had established the Norfolk Island settlement but was overlooked until he succeeded Governor Hunter in 1800. Instead, Lieutenant-Governor Francis Grose of the New South Wales Corps took charge and immediately set about making changes. His first act was to reduce rations to the convicts, thereby destroying Phillip's egalitarian ideals that officers should not receive more than convicts. He next overruled Phillip's insistence that the colony should not become a place for trade and that officers should not be rewarded simply for doing their duty; thus, he began to grant land and assign convicts as servants to officers of the Corps, paving the way for the corruption that followed. At the time, it was illegal for soldiers to engage in private trade while on duty, but this did little to stop the New South Wales Corps. Under the Corps the cost of goods skyrocketed and the penalties for crime became much harsher as military officers flaunted their powers. The Corps' control ushered in a period of stalled development in New South Wales until Governor Hunter took over and began issuing land grants in the Hawkesbury region. This region then became the colony's largest agricultural area until floods in 1809 encouraged settlers to move to the south-west area of Bringelly. Governors Hunter, King and Bligh all failed to curb the reckless ways of the Corps, a task left to Governor Macquarie in 1810. Bligh was unlucky in that he received little support from the colony's Judge-Advocate Richard Atkins, a renowned alcoholic who had once even pronounced a death sentence while drunk. Atkin's assistant, George Crossley, was a former English lawyer who had been sent to New South Wales for swindling and forgery; between the two of them, Bligh had little legal help.

MOVING INLAND

At the time of Governor Macquarie's arrival, Sydney's population stood at around 6200 people, with a further 2390 in the Hawkesbury region, 1810 in Parramatta and around 100 people in Newcastle. Of these, more than one-third were convicts. Free settlers had been slow in arriving but by 1805 the emigration of the wealthy Blaxland brothers began enticing other rich settlers to the colony. In 1817, Surveyor-General John Oxley explored land beyond the Cumberland Plains and Macquarie opened land up west of the Great Dividing Range — this sparked a push to settle the inland, including Goulburn and the Bredalbane Plains.

Above: Today's Sydney — it remains Australia's most populous city.

the FACTS!

IN 1794, Windsor on the Hawkesbury River replaced Parramatta as the biggest rural area in New South Wales.

SETTLEMENT along the New South Wales south coast began in the Shoalhaven District when Alexander Berry and Edward Wollstonecraft established a 6000 ha station in the area.

WHEN LT JOHN SHORTLAND found coal near the Hunter River in 1797, settlement of the Hunter Valley began. By 1801, coal was being worked in a penal colony that had been established at Newcastle, but was abandoned in 1802.

GOVERNOR MACQUARIE, a Scot, was accompanied by his men from the 73rd Regiment (the Second Black Watch) and they marched ashore to the sound of bagpipes. They wore new uniforms because kilts were inappropriate in the Australian sun.

IN 1816, free settlers were starting to be encouraged to migrate to NSW. Settlers were assigned 6–8 convicts to work for them. Assigning convicts as free labour for settlers meant that the government did not have to pay for their keep, but it also enticed free settlers to come.

GOVERNOR RALPH DARLING took control of New South Wales from 1825 to 1831.

IN 1826, the southern New South Wales Monaro tablelands were settled by squatters, the first of whom was Robert Campbell. In 1849, Cooma was surveyed.

Australian Capital Territory

Following Federation, Australia needed a new seat of Federal Parliament. The ACT was established with Canberra as the capital.

Left: **Robert Campbell built Duntroon House in 1853. It is now the officer's mess of the Royal Military College.**

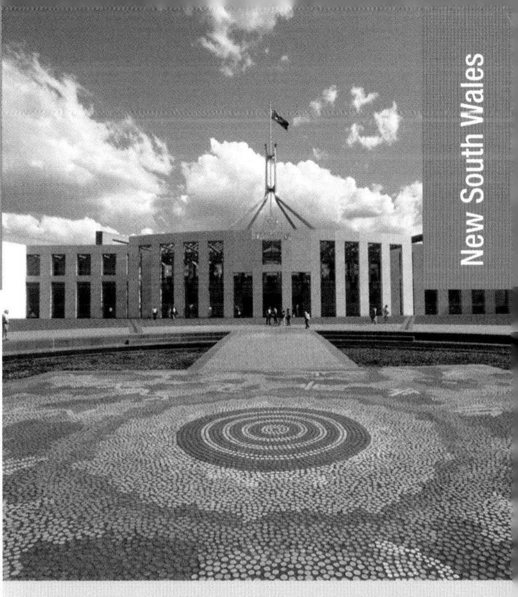

Above: **Parliament House in Canberra, the seat of Federal Government.**

BEYOND SYDNEY, gracious homesteads and cottages dotted the road to Bathurst, which by 1815 had established itself as a sizeable township. In the "Country of Cumberland", around Penrith, Camden and Windsor, recipients of the first land grants were now making a comfortable living. To the north, Maitland and Newcastle were growing, and eager settlers were moving further north from the New England Plains towards what would later become the Queensland border. Beyond the legal settlements of the colony, squatters pushed south-west to Gundagai, Young and Wagga. Governor Ralph Darling, who followed Governor Thomas Brisbane's reign (1821–1825) saw the end of the land grants system. By the time Governor Bourke came to office in 1831, Sydney was flourishing. Even Charles Darwin, who visited it in 1837, confessed he was "full of admiration" for the city. Trading firms and wealthy merchants, such as Simeon Lord, had constructed multi-level warehouses along George Street North and the banks of the Tank Stream. Affluent Sydneysiders dwelt in Hyde Park, Darlinghurst and Potts Point, while poorer people ran eclectic shops around the wharves at Sydney Cove and the Rocks.

PORT MACQUARIE

In 1821, a party of 40 solders, two officers' wives, four children and 60 convicts (under the command of Captain Allman) departed Sydney for Port Macquarie, which had been previously explored by John Oxley. There they were instructed to establish a penal settlement, which became an infamous hell hole for unreformed and incorrigible convicts. Despite its notoriety, Port Macquarie was also considered too easy to escape from to remain viable as a place of punishment, so by the time the convicts had been set to task clearing much of the timber from surrounding farmlands in the 1830s, it was opened to settlement. Settlers had, of course, already taken up land in the area and by 1829 most of the convicts had been moved to Moreton Bay or Norfolk Island. Only a small number of old, infirm or insane convicts remained at Port Macquarie prison, which was closed in 1847.

AN IMPORTANT PORT

By the 1820s, roads (many of which were built by convict labour) linked Sydney to Port Macquarie, Goulburn and Bathurst. However, the Sydney colony was very reliant on shipping and in 1803, Sydney's first commercial wharf was built. By 1811, Market Wharf in Darling Harbour had been constructed, followed in 1813 by the larger King's Wharf. Dawson's Foundry was established in 1833 as an iron works and, by 1837, more than 100 ships registered Sydney as their home port. A semi-circular quay was built around Sydney Cove by the 1850s.

Above: **Peaceful Port Macquarie is now a popular holiday town, but for many years it was a harsh penal settlement.** ***Right:*** **Mary Boulton's pioneer cottage in Macksville, New South Wales, was built in 1900 in the traditional slab hut style.**

the FACTS!

FROM 1787–1801, 43 transports departed England and Ireland for New South Wales. Combined, they carried 7486 prisoners, 756 of whom died at sea, often taking their last breath in chains in the stuffy darkness below deck.

BY 1814, the free wives of sentenced male convicts were able to travel in the transports to be with their husbands.

THE *SYDNEY GAZETTE* condescendingly observed in 1834, "*George Street, Parramatta, can now boast of some shops which would be worthy of observation and praise were they transferred to George Street, Sydney*".

BY 1835, the crime rate in the colony was reportedly eight times that of England. As a result death sentences more than doubled.

THE LAST CONVICT SHIP to New South Wales was supposed to arrive in 1840, but when the *Hashemy* arrived in 1849, there was rioting in the streets from those who believed transportation had stopped.

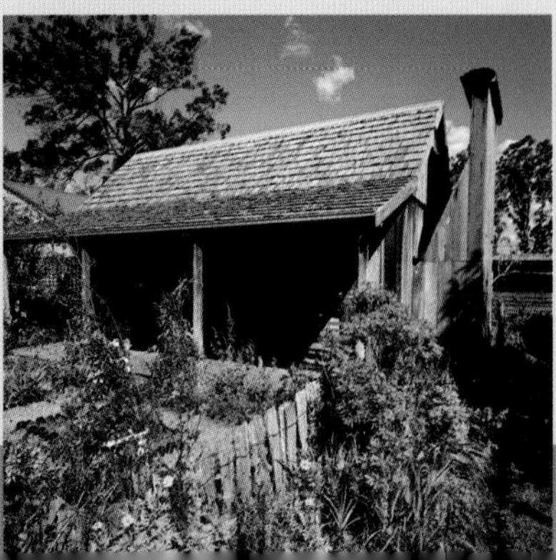

Van Diemen's Land

In 1642, Abel Tasman became the first European to sight the island that is now called Tasmania in his honour. However, the first settlement in Van Diemen's Land was only established under Governor King's term in 1803. It was established largely to stop French navigators such as D'Entrecasteaux and Baudin from trying to claim land for France.

Above: RG Reeve's depiction of Hobart Town was created in 1828.

the FACTS!

AMERICAN SEALERS and whalers began to establish camps in Van Diemen's Land before a penal colony was set up there.

WHEN EUROPEANS colonised Tasmania they offered the Tasmanian Aborigines fish, as was the custom in Port Jackson. The Aborigines refused it, to the dismay of the colonists. According to archaeological evidence, Aborigines in Tasmania stopped eating fish about 3000 years ago.

GOVERNMENT STORES were established on Hunters Island in Sullivans Cove to make it harder for convicts to steal supplies.

IN 1813, Colonel Thomas Davey became the lieutenant-governor for the whole island of Van Diemen's Land. Previously, both the Port Dalrymple and Hobart settlements had their own lieutenant-governors. One of his first acts was a proclamation to the Aboriginal people that showed drawings illustrating that both white men and Aborigines who murdered anyone would be hanged.

ON 12 SEPTEMBER 1803, Lieutenant John Bowen arrived with a small party at Risdon Cove on the Derwent River, naming the settlement Hobart, after Lord Hobart, Secretary of State of the colonies. When Lieutenant-Colonel David Collins, who had abandoned a site at Port Phillip in favour of Van Diemen's Land, arrived in February 1804, the settlement was moved to Sullivans Cove, where Hobart Town stands today. In its early years, Van Diemen's Land, as Tasmania was then known, was largely ignored by the British Government and received little assistance. Later, more convicts would be transported there than to any other Australian colony. Prisons to contain them were established at Sarah Island, Port Arthur and Maria Island and the most atrocious punishments were handed out in Van Diemen's Land's convict prisons.

SHANTY TOWN HOBART

When the new governor, Lachlan Macquarie, visited Hobart in 1811, he "observed with much regret" that the township was still little more than a conglomeration of shanty-like huts. He directed that it be immediately surveyed and set about authorising public works.

Above: Historic Victoria Dock, Hobart, today.

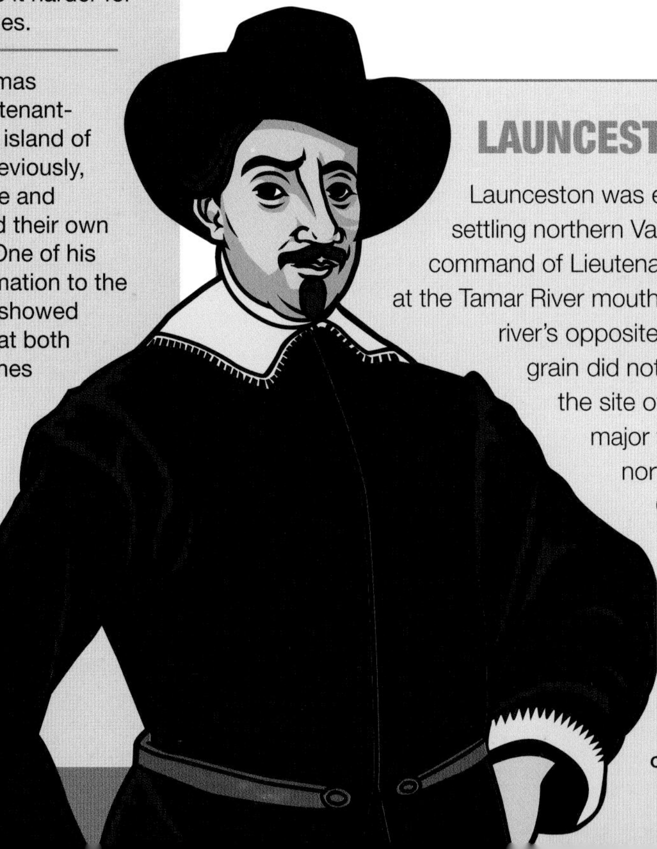

LAUNCESTON

Launceston was established in 1804 to deter the French from settling northern Van Diemen's Land. The HMS *Buffalo,* under the command of Lieutenant-Governor Paterson, landed in Port Dalrymple at the Tamar River mouth on 11 November. At first, York Town, on the river's opposite bank, was the intended settlement. However, grain did not grow well there so the settlement moved to the site of present day Launceston, named after the major town of Cornwall in England. At the time, northern Tasmania was referred to as the Colony of Cornwall. Launceston flourished as an industrial and commercial town and gold discoveries at Lefroy and Beaconsfield, and tin at Mt Bischoff in the 1860s, further increased Launceston's population.

Left: Abel Tasman named Tasmania Van Diemen's Land after Anthony Van Diemen (pictured), governor-general of Batavia and head of the Dutch East India Co.

Above, left to right: Saints & Sinners B&B in New Norfolk dates from 1845; Historic Highfield House at Stanley was built in 1832 and is the oldest house in north-west Tasmania; Richmond Bridge, over Coal River in Tasmania, was convict built and dates from 1825.

ALTHOUGH HOBART'S appearance improved after 1811 it remained a dangerous place. Free settlers first arrived in 1815, but when Governor William Sorrell arrived in 1817, convicts, both men and women, still roamed the streets at night vandalising buildings and engaging in drunken violence or illicit activities. However, the port was thriving. Whale oil, wool, wattle extract and seal skins left the port to be shipped around the globe and the whaling industry necessitated shipyards. By the late 1830s and early 1840s, Hobart constructed more ships than all other Australian ports put together and Battery Point became a crowded port-side village, packed with merchants, shipwrights and fishers.

A PUERILE PRISON

From 1824 to 1836, Van Diemen's Land was governed by Lieutenant-Governor George Arthur, who described child convicts there as "little depraved felons … thrown on the world, totally destitute". In the mid 1830s, he established Port Puer (meaning "Boy's Point") — a special prison for boys — near Port Arthur, south of present-day Hobart. By 1845, the prison held 730 boys, with the aim of reforming them through hard labour and training, mostly in trades. When the prison closed in 1849, more than 2000 young male inmates had passed through Port Puer — no boy ever managed to escape from the gaol.

PORT ARTHUR

In 1830, one of Australia's most notorious penal stations was established at Port Arthur on the windswept Tasman Peninsula. Its founder was Governor George Arthur, who took command in 1824. Arthur was a harsh man who was also responsible for the widespread relocation of Tasmania's Aboriginal population. By the late 1830s, life for convicts was increasingly tougher than it had been under Macquarie's leadership. Daily life at Norfolk Island and Port Arthur was so terrible that some convicts committed crimes in the hope that they would be executed — death being preferable to the torture inflicted in the penal colonies. In Van Diemen's Land, the chief superintendent of convicts wrote, *"any disobedience of orders, turbulence or other misconduct is instantaneously punished by the lash".*

Right, top to bottom: A menacing lion presides over ruins at Port Arthur; The most violent prisoners were kept locked up at the gaol; The Guard Tower.

the FACTS!

WHEN HUGH GERMAINE travelled Tasmania on foot in 1804 he took the *Bible* and *Arabian Nights* with him. Place names such as Bagdad and Jericho in Tasmania are allegedly named after those found in Germaine's reading material.

THE FIRST TRANSPORT to go direct from England to Hobart was the *Indefatigable*, which arrived with 199 convicts on board on 19 October 1812.

IN 1842, VAN DIEMEN'S LAND introduced a "probation gang" system where, after two years of work in a chain gang, well-behaved prisoners were given a probation pass and could work for wages. The convicts could later apply for a ticket of leave and finally a pardon.

IN 1846, FREE SETTLERS in Van Diemen's Land sent a petition to the House of Commons calling for an end to transportation. The petition also wanted more police protection for settlers.

VAN DIEMEN'S LAND separated from New South Wales in 1825, became the first Australian colony to be granted self-government in 1855 and was renamed Tasmania in 1856. It was thought that renaming the colony might help take the focus off the island's bloody, penal past.

Western Australian colony

Above: Major Edmund Lockyer settled King George Sound.

The first European known to have sighted Australia's west coast was Dutchman Dirk Hartog, who landed on Western Australian shores near Shark Bay by accident in 1616. Hartog left a plaque inscribed with the details of his voyage nailed to a tree.

IN SEPTEMBER 1791, George Vancouver discovered a harbour near modern-day Albany, which he named King George Sound. Later, the British Government — concerned that French explorers such as D'Entrecasteaux and Nicolas Baudin had been exploring the coast — instructed Governor Ralph Darling to start a settlement on the west coast. A small party was despatched to King George Sound, under the command of Major Edmund Lockyer, in 1826, but the remote settlement struggled to survive.

SWAN RIVER SETTLEMENT

In 1827, James Stirling and his men explored the Swan River, dragging boats across a sandbar in the river mouth to head upstream for 70 km. Stirling was impressed with what he saw and considered it a suitable place for a settlement. First, he attracted the interest of wealthy and influential English people prepared to help support a colony of free settlers. Only after the British Government saw the interest the new colony was creating among entrepreneurs did they decide to claim Western Australia as a British territory.

On 2 May 1829, Captain Charles Fremantle declared 2.5 million km^2 of Western Australia, the western third of the continent, as British land. Four weeks later, Stirling (who had been given the position of lieutenant-governor) arrived on the *Parmelia* along with his wife Ellen and two young children. Officers and soldiers of the 63rd Regiment, along with their families and other civil officials arrived on 6 June. Fremantle established a camp at the mouth of the Swan River, but Stirling moved further upriver and named it Perth on 12 August 1829. The original site at the river's mouth was named Fremantle.

Right, top to bottom: **Remnants of Western Australia's past preserved near New Norcia; The Round House gaol was convict built in 1831 and is the oldest surviving building in Western Australia. In 1837, a tunnel beneath it was dug to allow whalers to access the town.**

LAND LURES SETTLERS

At first, 40 acres could be granted for every £3 of capital the settler owned, which could be a pension, farming tools or livestock. Settlers were also granted an extra 200 acres for each worker they paid to travel to the colony with them. Land in New South Wales at the time was selling for £10 for 40 acres.

By April 1830, more than 1500 immigrants had arrived at Swan River, ready to begin a new life. Some of the settlers, such as Robert Peel (the cousin of the English prime minister) and the Henty brothers (who brought 33 servants with them), were wealthy settlers who wanted to make a

the **FACTS!**

ARCHAEOLOGISTS ESTIMATE that Aborigines lived on the Upper Swan River at least 34,000 years ago. There were around 90 Aboriginal groups living in Western Australia before settlement.

PHILLIP PARKER KING charted much of the north-west coast of Western Australia on his ships the *Mermaid* and *Bathurst*.

GOVERNOR STIRLING wanted to call the colony "Hesperia", after the evening star.

EXPLORATION around Perth followed settlement, with Lt Henry exploring the Canning River in 1829 and Lt William Preston and Alexander Collie surveying land to the south later the same year.

WEALTHY THOMAS PEEL paid for several settlers to emigrate, thus helping settle Perth. In return for his help, Peel was granted a large tract of land by the British Government.

WESTERN AUSTRALIA'S first pastoral region was settled in the Avon Valley in the early 1840s.

THE *HOUGOUMONT* was the last convict ship to arrive in Australia, reaching Fremantle on 9 January 1868 with a cargo of 279 prisoners.

Above: George Pitt Morrison's oil painting *The Foundation of Perth* shows Mrs Dance, wife of Captain William Dance, preparing to strike a tree to declare the site of Perth.

Above: Captain James Stirling.

fortune in the new land. Favourable reports of the colonies flooded the newspapers. One article entitled *Hints on Emigration* instructed, "*Take a three-roomed prefabricated wooden house with you. Two workmen can assemble it for you in 24 hours. The climate is like the best parts of Europe. There is no need for previous experience. A man will be able to support his family in a couple of months*".

However, when settlers arrived they found the settlement was far from what they expected. There wasn't a proper port, so immigrants had to dump their goods over the side above the tideline. Drinking water and food were scarce, sandflies and mosquitoes were rife, and the area lacked suitable food and water for livestock. Conditions were not sanitary and many people died of dysentery. Well-brought-up ladies had to muck in with the servants to carry buckets of water, unload stores and grow vegetables. One horrified newcomer wrote, "They walk around with nothing on their feet like gypsies".

MINERAL WEALTH

Western Australia is now known to be a place of enormous mineral wealth and many a man has made his fortune there. In 1855, gold was discovered in Halls Creek in the Kimberley. Further discoveries were made in the Pilbara region in 1888 and around the Murchison River from 1890, before Australia's greatest gold rush began in Coolgardie in 1892.

For the next decade, towns such as Coolgardie and nearby Kalgoorlie would see Western Australia flourish. Some settlers capitalised on other natural resources found in the area, such as sandalwood, jarrah timber and whale oil.

WE NEED CONVICTS!

At first, the Swan River colony faltered and grew slowly. Soon, people in Perth gathered to actively demand that Swan River become a convict colony because they needed the free labour to support the colony. The British Government had ended transportation to New South Wales and once more faced overflowing gaols, hence the first shipload of 75 convicts arrived in Swan River by 1 June 1850. By this time, transportation to most of the other settlements had ceased.

Transportation continued for the next eighteen years and brought an influx of 10,000 convicts to Western Australia. All of the prisoners sent to Western Australia were men and most of them were not hardened criminals.

the FACTS!

GOVERNOR JOHN HUTT was instructed in 1839 to fine settlers who had not planted crops on their land, despite the sandy soil and labour shortage making farming difficult. The price of land was also increased, meaning that many settlers were reluctant to settle in Western Australia when they could buy more fertile land elsewhere.

JOHN SEPTIMUS ROE, Western Australia's first surveyor-general, was also the first European to explore the great salt lakes in 1835.

JOHN FORREST (who later become the first premier of Western Australia) and his brother Alexander, forged the path for the construction of a telegraph line through WA.

TRANSPORTATION HELPED quadruple the colony's population, but even in 1868 only 24,000 Europeans called Swan River home.

THE STATE'S POPULATION did not grow significantly until the early 1900s — it skyrocketed to 239,000 people in 1904.

PERTH'S PEARLS

Pearling began in Western Australia in 1861, but did not become a thriving industry until the 1880s, when pearl-buttons came into fashion and Broome became the hub of the State's pearling industry. In the early days, Aboriginal women were captured and forced to dive for pearls — a dangerous and sometimes fatal task, which could result in being killed by sharks or suffering the bends. Later, Japanese and Malaysian divers wore helmeted canvas suits to protect them while underwater, but many still died. Between 1909 and 1917, 145 divers died from the bends.

Above: Stone settlers' cottages dot the State — this one is near Renmark, SA.

A free State — South Australia

The Dutch first spied the coast of what would later become South Australia in 1627, when Captain François Thijssen and Pieter Nuyts sailed along the Great Australian Bight to what is now known as Nuyts Archipelago, near Ceduna.

LATER, IN 1802–1803, navigator Matthew Flinders circumnavigated Australia and made a complete survey of South Australia's coast, on the way "encountering" French navigator Nicolas Baudin at Encounter Bay. Later, overland explorers made extensive forays into South Australia. In 1831, Captain Collet Barker explored Gulf St Vincent, Mount Lofty and Port Adelaide before trekking overland to discover a route from Lake Alexandrina (the mouth of the Murray) to Encounter Bay. Eight years later, Edward Eyre and Wylie, his Aboriginal guide, explored land north of Spencer Gulf and travelled from Port Lincoln to Streaky Bay, returning via the Gawler Range and Lake Torrens.

WAKEFIELD'S SUGGESTION

The plan for South Australia's colonisation was devised by English Quaker Edward Gibbon Wakefield (who had never been to Australia!). Rather than granting land to ex-convicts, he suggested it should be sold to free settlers and the money used to pay for poor settlers of good character to farm more land; after farming it for some time they would have the option to buy it. Supporters urged the British Government to adopt the plan. The government agreed, on the proviso that the land would raise at least £35,000. On the 15 August 1834, the *South Australian Colonisation Act* decreed that land was to be sold at a minimum of twelve shillings an acre. Colonel Robert Torrens controlled land sales and the money was raised by the end of 1835. No one who had bought the land had actually seen it.

A SETTLEMENT OF SEALERS

In the early 1800s, sealing and whaling were extremely lucrative industries. British and American merchant ships that brought settlers or goods to the colony usually tried to return home with a cargo of whale baleen or seal skins to fund their voyage. When Nicolas Baudin, who had explored Kangaroo Island in 1803, met with the captain of Amercian sealing ship the *Union* off the Western Australian coast, he told them of the abundant seals on Kangaroo Island in South Australia. When the *Union* arrived there, the crew were so astounded by the profit to be made that half of them remained on the island to build another boat, while the other half set about slaughtering seals — giving rise to the town named American River on Kangaroo Island. From 1805, ships sailing from Tasmania regularly dropped sealers on the island for the seal season. A small settlement was well-established on Kangaroo Island by the time Colonel Light arrived there in the *Rapid* on 19 August 1836. However, Colonel Light did not find the island a suitable place for a settlement. Instead he went in search of land that was fertile, close to suitable building materials and had plenty of fresh water. By 1927, up to 40 men lived permanently on Kangaroo Island. Today, Australia's seals are protected and many thousands of tourists visit Kangaroo Island to admire these playful, friendly creatures.

the FACTS!

ABOUT twenty Aboriginal groups (a total of 10,000 to 14,000 people) lived in South Australia when European settlers arrived, including the Ngarrindjeri, Pitjantjatjara, Kaurna and Wangkangurru peoples.

THE BRITISH GOVERNMENT, in planning South Australia, said that 20% of the money raised from land sales would be used to buy land for the Aboriginal people. Unfortunately, this rarely happened and most of the Aboriginal peoples who had lived around Adelaide were displaced.

IN 1835, the South Australian Company was formed in London under the directorship of George Fife Angas. Its aim was to garner British investment in colonising South Australia, in conjunction with the UK Government. The following year, the company set up a whaling station on Kangaroo Island and another at Encounter Bay in 1837. Whaling stations later sprang up at Port Elliot Bay and Victor Harbor.

IN 1838 German Lutherans, fleeing religious persecution, began arriving at Port Adelaide. By 1842, they had settled Kelmzig, Lobethal and Hahndorf (below), as well as Bethany in the Barossa Valley.

Above, left to right: Adelaide's square city grid seen from the air; Glenelg, then called Holdfast Bay, was where the first settlers landed.

LIGHT YEARS AHEAD

In 1836, Malaysian-born Colonel Wiliam Light (left) was appointed surveyor-general of the new Province of South Australia. His plan was based around a grid of wide, square streets with plenty of parklands, a hospital, cemetery, government stores and offices. Even suffering from tuberculosis, Light managed to survey 150,000 acres and plan the city by 1838. He died of his illness on 6 October 1839, before his vision was fully realised, but to this day Adelaide remains one of the best planned and most spacious Australian capitals.

THE FIRST EUROPEAN SETTLERS in the free colony of South Australia arrived at Holdfast Bay (now Glenelg) in 1836 aboard the HMS *Buffalo* under the command of Captain John Hindmarsh. They landed on 28 December — the day South Australians celebrate as Proclamation Day, but soon realised that 300 settlers had already arrived upon whaling ships under the command of the South Australia Company. Later, Colonel William Light proposed to move the settlement to the banks of the Torrens River, although Hindmarsh disagreed, believing that Encounter Bay, near the Murray mouth, was a better option. The city was named Adelaide after Queen Adelaide, King William IV of England's wife. Debate about the city's location continued until George Gawler replaced Hindmarsh as governor in 1838.

When Gawler arrived in October 1838, he began to set up public works. His aim was to create employment by building roads and government buildings using clay bricks and limestone. By 1842, about 500,000 acres had been surveyed and vineyards, hobby farms and market gardens had sprung up close to town.

IMMIGRANTS & INDUSTRY

Many thousands of immigrants (most younger than 30 years of age) were paid to emigrate to South Australia. Although the government promised them jobs, unemployment was high until copper was discovered near Burra. Outside of the city, sheep, cattle and wheat farms were established. Wheat quickly became the State's biggest export. Labour shortages followed as settlers became able to afford to buy their own plots rather than work for landholders. A shortage of labour for the wheat harvest in 1843 meant that the government had to supply troops to work!

GOYDER'S LINE

George Goyder believed he had found a pastoralist's Eden around Lake Blanch, but he had visited it in the wet season; in the dry season the area was arid and barren. When, as surveyor-general, Goyder later surveyed the countryside following the droughts of 1864–1865, he became convinced that some of the land was useless for farming. On a map of the State, he marked an area where rainfall was insufficient for farming and set the limits of settlement within the arable area. This became known as Goyder's line and played an important role in South Australia's pattern of settlement.

Right: This plaque was erected at Terowie and depicts Goyder's Line.

the FACTS!

ADELAIDE'S REPUTATION as a city of churches was in place by 1857 — there were already around 300 churches or chapels in the city. Elegant St Peter's Cathedral (below) dates from 1901.

THE MURRAY RIVER was crucial to the settlement of South Australia, but didn't provide an economical method of transport until 1853, when the first steam-powered riverboat, the *Lady Augusta*, sailed from Sydney to Goolwa, and up the Murray to Swan Hill in Victoria.

SOUTH AUSTRALIA became a separate colony in 1842 and wheat and mineral wealth from copper, discovered in 1845, became its major exports. By 1850, around 38,000 immigrants had arrived. Although it was never a convict colony, some convicts and ex-convicts did settle there.

IN 1866, camels were shipped from India to Port Augusta and Afghan cameleers arrived to drive teams for inland explorers. By 1901, about 400 Afghan cameleers made Australia home. In honour of these stalwarts of the desert, the Ghan Railway, built in 1929, was named after these Afghan traders.

Above: Collins Street, Melbourne, circa 1895.

Victoria — "Hell or Melbourne"

Lieutenant John Murray, sailing the Lady Nelson *in 1802, was the first person to sail into Port Phillip Bay. Later the same year, Charles Grimes was sent, in the* Cumberland, *to monitor the progress of French ships. In 1803, Colonel David Collins accompanied a party of convicts to found a new Port Phillip colony.*

HUTS, A WELL AND STORES were constructed near Sorrento, but the colony was later abandoned and moved to Van Diemen's Land.

A whaling station was established in Portland Bay in the 1830s, and gradually word spread of the lush grazing land available. Squatters such as the Henty brothers began to arrive from 1834. Entrepreneurs were eager for the spoils that the new land could bring, and in 1835 John Batman set off to explore Port Philip Bay's western shores on behalf of wealthy landowners, such as Joseph Gellibrand, who were seeking arable land for squatting. Batman struck up an infamous "treaty" with the Aborigines, later writing:

> *I purchased two large blocks of tracts of land, about 600,000 acres, more or less, and, in consideration there for, I gave them blankets, knives, looking-glasses, tomahawks, beads, scissors, flour &c., and I also further agreed to pay them a tribute or rent yearly. The parchment or deed was signed this afternoon by eight chiefs, each of them at the same time, handing me a portion of the soil: thus giving me full possession of the tracts of land I had purchased.*

However, when Batman returned to Van Diemen's Land, Governor Arthur refused to accept his land purchase. Governor Bourke, of New South Wales, insisted that anyone settling Port Phillip was trespassing, but this did nothing to stop eager investors from moving to the Port Phillip District.

Above: Melbourne Wharf, looking south-west from Custom's House in 1853. *Right*: Archaeological evidence suggests Aborigines inhabited the Port Phillip district for at least 31,000 years before Batman's infamous treaty occurred. Governor Arthur refused to accept Batman's treaty with the Aborigines, but settlers later flocked to the area anyway.

the FACTS!

ON 24 APRIL 1803, Lt David Collins commanded the *Calcutta* and the storeship *Ocean* on an expedition to found a new settlement at Port Phillip. The ships carried male convicts and 37 wives and children, but the site was quickly deemed unsuitable and, in 1804, Collins moved the settlement to Van Diemen's Land.

AS EARLY AS 1798, George Bass noted that sealers had already begun to colonise the Bass Strait Islands off Victoria's coast.

JOHN PASCOE FAWKNER, one of the founding fathers of Melbourne, first landed on Victorian soil as an eleven-year-old. He was the son of a convict transported for fourteen years and was among the wives and children David Collins took to Port Phillip aboard the *Calcutta*.

THE SETTLEMENT established by Batman and Fawkner was little more than a tent city. Settlers argued about a suitable name for the new colony. Batman favoured "Batmania", but it was officially named Melbourne in 1837.

JOHN BATMAN, one of the founders of Melbourne, was hired to seek out bushrangers and "bolters" in Van Diemen's Land in the early 1800s. He hadn't anticipated finding a woman, but when he found Eliza Callaghan, who had escaped from gaol for the fourth time, he hid her and later married her in 1825.

SETTLER SHIPS began to arrive, bringing hopeful immigrants to Victoria, but conditions on them were awful. "Hell or Melbourne" was the motto on one of the ships bringing out first settlers to Melbourne.

Above: Melbourne is a thriving, vibrant metropolis today. In the 1860s it was the fastest-growing city in the world and, by 1877, Victoria's population surpassed that of New South Wales, with approximately 818,935 people to 642,845 in New South Wales.

SETTLERS ARRIVE

In August 1835, John Pascoe Fawkner sailed up the Yarra River, divided up land for some investors and free settlers and began to farm. More settlers quickly followed and Fawkner and his family opened a hotel. Batman ignored Governor Bourke's declaration and followed. Approximately 177 European settlers, running 26,000 sheep had arrived in the Port Phillip District by May 1836, leaving Governor Bourke little choice but to declare settlement of the area open.

Graziers and drovers began arriving from New South Wales, following in the tracks of explorers such as Hovell and Hume, Thomas Mitchell and Angus McMillan. It was a long and dangerous journey of more than 1000 km and those who undertook it faced risks from bushrangers, Aborigines, and the elements.

In 1837–1838, men such as Charles Bonney and Joseph Hawdon began to drive their stock across country to market at Adelaide, a hazardous three month journey. Six years later, in 1844, a trading route based on Angus McMillan's exploration route linked Melbourne with Gippsland, avoiding the mountain ranges.

MARVELLOUS MELBOURNE

Once Melbourne was surveyed in 1837, brick and bluestone buildings were constructed, along with mills, warehouses and merchants' stores. By 1842, a council was established to supervise drainage, road building, markets and street lighting, and Melbourne began to be recognised as a flourishing town. By 1851 Melbourne had a population of 29,000.

The discovery of gold in Warrandyte, Clunes and Buninyong (near Ballarat) later that same year only added to the influx of settlers. The population increased dramatically following the gold rush, more than doubling to reach 1.2 million by 1890. Over half of the fortune-hunters chose to stay on in Melbourne, and, although government incentives for immigration ceased in 1873, immigrants continued to flock to Victoria. By 1891, "Marvellous Melbourne" was the 22nd-largest city in the world and Victoria also boasted another 120 towns that had populations of more than 500. Most of these towns had at least one blacksmith, butcher, bank, general store, school, hotel, church, post office and railway station. Larger towns had their own town hall, public gardens and newspaper.

the FACTS!

SOME OF VICTORIA'S earliest settlers were John and Peter Manifold, who settled near Geelong in 1836 and later developed Camperdown.

CAPTAIN WILLIAM LONSDALE was despatched from Sydney in 1837 to take on the role of police magistrate of Port Phillip, but was replaced by Charles La Trobe, as superintendent, in 1839. La Trobe was later promoted to lieutenant-governor in 1840 and Victoria was declared a separate colony in 1851.

IN MELBOURNE and Williamstown, crown land was first sold at a cost of £35 per half acre on 1 June 1837.

GOVERNOR LA TROBE'S cottage (below) was carefully shipped out from England in sections — it now stands in the Domain parklands of Melbourne.

Moreton Bay
& Queensland

New South Wales Surveyor John Oxley (left) explored Moreton Bay in 1823, naming the wide river he found there the Brisbane, after Governor Sir Thomas Brisbane. On 10 September 1824, the Moreton Bay penal settlement was established at Redcliffe under the command of Henry Miller, but, after being besieged by mosquitoes, was moved to the site of North Quay in present-day Brisbane in February 1825.

the FACTS!

THE JAGERA AND TURRBAL Aboriginal people are the traditional owners of land around Brisbane.

JOHN OXLEY was alerted to the existence of the Brisbane River by two ex-convicts, Pamphlett and Finnegan, who had been living with Aborigines near Bribie Island.

MORETON BAY was originally called Morton's Bay by Captain Cook in 1770, but was later misspelt and became Moreton Bay.

BRISBANE'S name was officially Edinglassie, but no one called it that. Aborigines called it *Meanjin*.

BETWEEN 1824–1839 around 2280 convicts were sent to the walled gaol of Moreton Bay — one of the harshest penal prisons.

THE OLD WINDMILL at Wickham Terrace was convict built in 1828–1829. An official report of convict deaths written in 1829 records that one convict, Michael Collins, was "entangled in the machinery of the tread wheel and killed".

Below: Brisbane, seen beyond the Story Bridge, is now one of the fastest-growing capitals in Australia.

BUILT BY PRISONERS

The settlement that would later go on to become Brisbane, Queensland's capital, was literally convict built. In 1828, hundreds of convicts were sent there to add to the existing ten cottages by building stone constructions such as the colonial stores building and the old windmill on Wickham Terrace. Farms were also set up at Bundamba, Eagle Farm and New Farm. Captain Patrick Logan, a much-feared disciplinarian, took command of Moreton Bay from 1825 and penal settlements at Stradbroke Island and Limestone (Ipswich) were established by 1827. The colony contained only the most hardened prisoners and Captain Logan worked them cruelly before he was eventually murdered and found buried in a shallow grave in 1834. He was succeeded by James Clunie. In 1839, the convict era ended and in 1841 Governor George Gipps surveyed a site for Brisbane. Town lots went on sale for £343 an acre. The surrounding district was opened for settlement in 1842.

AN INAUDIBLE SQUEAK

Initially, Brisbane was comprised of three separate settlements — Kangaroo Point, North Brisbane and South Brisbane. The colony grew slowly and by 1846 the three areas combined had a population of fewer than 1000 people. Authorities in New South Wales were reluctant to provide funds for improvements to Brisbane Town and Brisbanites lamented that "the voice of the Moreton Bay people amounted to only a very inaudible squeak". However, Brisbane was determined to succeed, if not under the control of New South Wales, then as a colony in its own right. The *Moreton Bay Courier* in 1847 demanded that "our feet shall stand upon the same political level as other colonists ...

Above, left to right: In 1883, horses and carts clattered down what is now the Queen Street Mall. Most of Brisbane's grand architecture such as Old Government House, the Mansions and Customs House was under construction during this decade; In 1846, pastoralist Patrick Leslie financed the construction of Newstead House, Brisbane's oldest surviving residence.

For this cause the inhabitants are banding together … they may fall but they will never surrender". But the rebuttal from Sydney was derisory. The *Sydney Morning Herald* scathingly wrote "It is difficult to mete out the proportions of laughter, pity and contempt which must be awarded to our fellow-colonists lying to the northward". However, the British Government disagreed and on 10 December 1859 Moreton Bay was declared a separate colony, under the command of Governor George Bowen, and was renamed Queensland in honour of Queen Victoria.

Above, left to right: St Helena Island in Moreton Bay was a floating prison for convicts; Governor Thomas Brisbane, for whom Brisbane is named.

FORTITUDE VALLEY

When Scottish free settlers who arrived on the SS *Fortitude* in 1849 discovered that the free land grants they had been promised were unavailable, some of them set up camp in Bowen Hills, naming it Fortitude Valley after the ship they had arrived on.

Fortitude Valley would go on to be a major commercial precinct with the establishment of the huge TC Beirne and McWhirters department stores. Following floods in 1893 and 1897 many merchants from South Brisbane also moved their stores to the Valley, which was accessible from the city by train and horse-drawn tram.

Above: Shopping in Wickham Street, Fortitude Valley, in 1908. *Below:* Wickham Street today.

the FACTS!

SETTLEMENT AROUND the penal colony was limited to within 80 km of Brisbane Town at first, but people began to squat in the district from 1838. In 1840, Patrick Leslie drove sheep to the Darling Downs, where he profited from a large run on the Condamine River. Soon, more than 45 stations were shipping bales of wool from the region, even before it was declared open for settlement.

ABORIGINES Dalinkua and Dalpie from the Breakfast Creek area wrote to the *Moreton Bay Courier* in 1858 condemning the way the settlers treated their people.

BY THE TIME Queensland was declared in 1859, graziers had settled most of the State from the Fitzroy River to the Darling Downs.

WHEN THE FIRST GOVERNOR of Queensland, Sir George Bowen, took up his tenure, he found he had just 7.5 pence in the treasury — within two days even that had been stolen!

BRISBANE'S convict-built heritage was replaced with grand buildings such as Customs House and Old Government House by 1888.

DURING the late 19th century, commerce in Brisbane was divided by religion. Catholic shops were in Stanley Street, South Brisbane, while Protestant shops lined Queen and Adelaide Streets in the city.

Above: Browns Mart is the oldest commercial building in Darwin, dating from 1885.

Northern Territory — a trading base

The northern coast of Australia was first seen by Dutch navigator Willem van Colster as early as 1623, but it was the last region to be settled by Europeans, who struggled to survive tropical diseases, unpredictable weather and attacks by Aborigines.

FOUR ATTEMPTS WERE made to found settlements in the 1800s, but all were quickly abandoned. Many factors contributed to the failure of the early settlements, including their isolation and the fact that they were not on any established trading routes. Hot, humid weather and frequent storms and cyclones, along with poor soil and plagues of insects, destroyed crops. Tropical diseases carried by the abundant mosquitoes also killed many of the settlers. Those that survived the diseases were under threat from Aborigines and from the large crocodiles that patrolled the waterways (right).

Right: Remote Port Essington, as depicted by Edwin Augustus Porcher's watercolour in 1845.

FORTS AND FAILURES

With the intention of opening a trade route with Indonesia, Captain Bremer was sent to settle Fort Dundas, on Melville Island, in September 1824. The settlement was unsuccessful — in part due to the persistence of the Tiwi Aborigines, who fiercely resisted occupation — and was abandoned by January 1829.

On 17 June 1827, Captain James Stirling tried to establish Fort Wellington at Raffles Bay. Although Stirling had better provisions than Bremer, this settlement also failed in 1829. However, Captain Collet Barker, who had taken command in 1828, was reluctant to quit because he was convinced it was possible with more perseverance. Captain Bremer was to be given a second chance when asked to set up Fort Victoria at Port Essington in October 1838, but it too was deserted by 1849. It was an unsuitable site, later described by Thomas Huxley as "*... most wretched, the climate the most unhealthy, the human beings the most uncomfortable and houses in a condition most decayed and rotten*".

Rash Lieutenant-Colonel Boyle Finniss was appointed to establish a colony at Escape Cliffs, 75 km from Darwin, in 1864, but with one of his first orders being to "shoot every b—y native you see", it was little wonder that violence between the settlers and the Aborigines thwarted the settlement's chance of success and the Escape Cliffs colony was abandoned by 1867.

Below: Frenchman Emile Lassalle's impression of the Raffles Bay settlement, Fort Wellington.

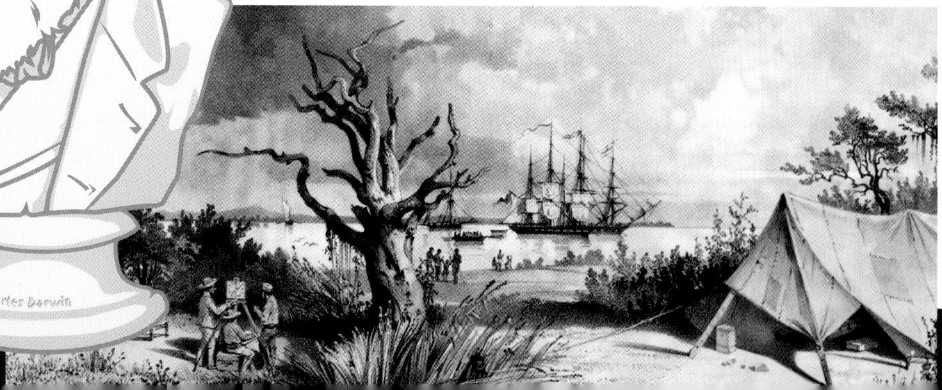

the FACTS!

APPROXIMATELY 35,000 Aboriginal people living in 126 different groups inhabited the Northern Territory before European occupation.

THE NORTHERN TERRITORY was initially part of New South Wales when first settled in September 1824. However, in 1863, it officially became part of South Australia, which governed the Territory until 1911 when the Commonwealth Government took over administration.

ARNHEM LAND (below) was named after Willem van Colster's ship, the *Arnhem*.

GOLD DISCOVERIES at Grove Hill in 1872, Pine Creek, Burrundi and Brocks Creek brought eager prospectors to the Territory.

IN 1978, the Northern Territory was granted self government.

IN 1839, the HMS *Beagle,* in which esteemed evolutionist Charles Darwin (right) had travelled, visited Port Essington. The town of Darwin is named after this famous scientist.

Right: Bust of Charles Darwin.

Above: The Old Police Station and Courthouse in Darwin. Many of Darwin's colonial buildings were destroyed in cyclone Tracy on 25 December 1974 or by World War II bombing.

HUGE STATIONS, HUGE DEBTS

The first unsuccessful forays into Northern Australia deterred further efforts until explorer John McKinlay recommended a site he named Port Darwin as a place for a city. Pastoralists, heartened by Augustus Gregory's discovery of rich pastures around Victoria River, began to seek good grazing lands in what became known as "Centralia" and soon moved northwards from South Australia into the Territory. By the 1880s, graziers hoped to support thousands of animals on huge leased properties, but many later went bankrupt when they discovered that the shallow soil would not support pasture grasses year round. Those that profited owe much of their success to Aboriginal labour.

A NORTHERN CAPITAL

In 1869, Palmerston (which would later be renamed Darwin) was established. The driving force behind Darwin was the extension of the Overland Telegraph Line to Java in 1870, via a submarine cable. The South Australian government funded the line's construction from Adelaide to Darwin and at last the lonely northern outpost was connected with the rest of the nation. This, coupled with a short gold rush at Pine Creek, increased the Territory's appeal.

Many of the Chinese who settled around Darwin following the gold rush remained and added to the lively multicultural mix in the city today. Aborigines make up more than 22% of the population of the Northern Territory and have legal title to many of their traditional lands in the Top End, including Kakadu and Uluṟu–Kata Tjuṯa National Parks.

Above: Darwin wharf in the 1880s.

Below: Boats moored in Darwin Harbour today.

Land of the ancients

More than 50% of the Northern Territory is Aboriginal land or is under Native Title claims.

the **FACTS!**

ALFRED GILES and Alfred Woods drove stock to Katherine, where they built Springvale Homestead in 1879. It is the oldest remaining homestead in the Northern Territory and is open to the public.

ALICE SPRINGS was first named Stuart in 1888. It was renamed in 1933 after the wife of Telegraph Supervisor Sir Charles Todd.

IN 1838–1839, under the "Kimberley Scheme", parts of the Territory were under consideration as a site for a potential Jewish homeland. Most people scoffed at the idea and suggested it be called the "Unpromised Land".

WHEN PRIME MINISTER Alfred Deakin agreed to transfer the Territory to the Commonwealth in 1911, he said, "Either we must accomplish the peopling of the Northern Territory or submit to its transfer to some other nation".

AUSTRALIA'S last gold rush was at Tennant Creek in the 1930s.

THE NORTHERN TERRITORY is the only State in Australia to have ever been placed under military government. This happened during World War II when Darwin was bombed and the Top End was a vital military base for troops. After the war, the Commonwealth Government again took command.

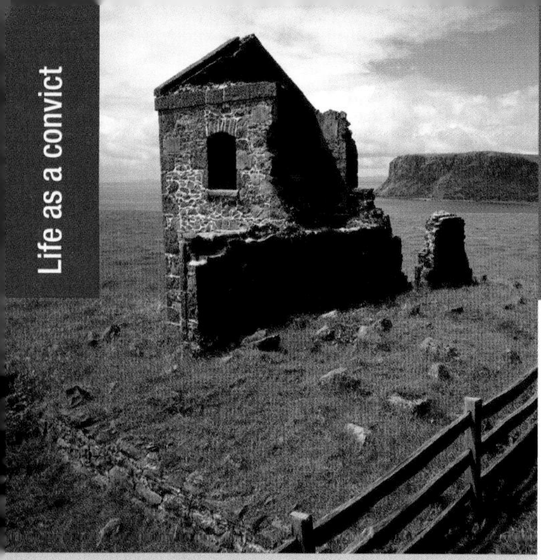

Above: Remnants of a women's prison, near The Nut, Stanley, Tasmania.

Convict life in the colonies

Treatment of convicts varied from colony to colony, although most historians agree that those that arrived in the early days of Australia's settlement usually had a much easier life than those transported to Australia after the Third Fleet.

CONVICT LABOUR

In New South Wales in 1819, most convicts worked in quarries and lumber yards, constructed buildings, built ports and repaired boats. Some male convicts worked in chain gangs, building and repairing roads, others worked on government farms or as timber-getters. Squatters also took on some convict shepherds and stationhands. Undesirable jobs were working in the coal mines or limestone pits. Women felons were usually employed as dairy maids, nannies or domestic staff.

LAUGHING IT OFF

Sometimes, having a good sense of humour and being able to make a guard or policeman laugh could be the difference between death or release. One notoriously comedic convict, known as Billy Blue (above right), was several times released for the inventive excuses he gave for his crimes. After being caught smuggling alcohol he told authorities that he was unlucky enough to just keep finding alcohol floating in Sydney Harbour and was caught with it before he could report it to the police. The authorities accepted his very unlikely explanation and he was not gaoled. He later befriended Governor Macquarie.

FEMALE FACTORIES

At first, some female convicts lived in private lodgings while others were immediately granted tickets of leave; however, later in the colonies, special accommodation was built to help reform convict women and teach them useful skills. In 1804, the first female factory was built at Parramatta (below). Here, women and girls were taught to spin and knit wool, make clothes and domestic goods such as brooms and utensils, and perform other domestic tasks, with some eventually taking up jobs as scullery maids and servants for government officials. Many convict women, however, remained of base character. In 1838, the Report of the Select Committee on Transportation, somewhat unfairly stated that women convicts were *"all of them, with scarcely an exception, drunken and abandoned prostitutes … It can be easily imagined what a pernicious effect must be produced on the character of the rising generation under the charge of such persons"*.

the FACTS!

IN 1804, convicts began to be assigned to work for settlers and officers. If they were assigned to a generous master, they might be rewarded for hard work with luxuries such as tea and tobacco. D'Arcy Wentworth was particularly kind to the convicts who were assigned to him. On the contrary, James Mudie, of Castle Forbes in the Hunter Valley, was the target of murder attempts for his harsh reputation.

CONVICT MECHANICS were highly sought after because *"a convict who has been a blacksmith, carpenter, mason, cooper, wheelwright or gardener is a most valuable servant worth three or four ordinary convicts"*.

SOME CONVICTS who married free settlers, or whose free spouses had arrived with them on the transports, were lucky enough to be assigned to their spouse.

"THE GOVERNMENT STROKE" was considered the eight hours a day government convicts worked. After those eight hours had finished, usually by 1–3 pm, male convicts were able to hire themselves out for wages. Convicts who did this were known as "government men".

IN 1838, regulations stipulated that assigned convicts must receive "two frocks or jackets, two pair of trousers, three pair of shoes and a hat" annually.

Above: Building roads in "road gangs" involved smashing up and removing heavy rocks and digging up a roadway.

Frankie the poet

Francis MacNamara was a popular convict poet. However he (along with other outspoken convicts) was regularly flogged for writing ballads that criticised the authorities.

SONGS FOR THE SOULLESS

Origins of traditional Australian folk music began with convicts, who would sing songs or write ballads lamenting their situation or chastising their masters. As the colony expanded, convict poems grew into folk songs such as *Bound for Botany Bay, Maggie May, Convict Maid, Bound for South Australia, Van Diemen's Land, Jim Jones* and *Moreton Bay*. Often convict composers were flogged for writing ballads that were dismissive of the establishment or that criticised their captors. Some tunes were even banned — but this usually led to variations of them being developed and sung in rebellious chorus. Edgar Waters noted that despite punishments given for encouraging dissent, "the convicts could not be stopped from singing".

A FATE WORSE THAN DEATH

Some colonies were much harsher on convicts than others. Life at Moreton Bay penal colony in the 1820s was so demoralising that one convict, Jack Bushman, relayed the following conversation to a newspaper journalist:

> *Working one day on the … road … there was a prisoner named Tom Allen, and a Scotch [sic] boy by his side. I call the last named a boy, as he was so young, though he had apparently grown up. I give the scene exactly as it occurred:*
> *'I am tired of life', said Tom Allen.*
> *'So am I,' answered the boy.*
> *'I will kill you if you like,' responded Tom, 'then they will hang me, and there will an end to both of us.'*
> *'Do so,' spoke the boy. Tom raised the pick he was using, struck the boy on the head … the boy's life was gone.*
>
> *As Tom finished his bloody deed, he exclaimed, 'So, we are now both dead men'.*

Above: Some convicts were set to work on "tramways", pulling wheeled carts over the unpaved roads.

NO DETERRENT?

Despite some convicts preferring death to a convict life, the 1838 report of the Select Committee on Transportation found that transportation was not a deterrent for criminals nor did it reform them, although it was "*... not a simple punishment, but rather a series of punishments, embracing every degree of human suffering, from the lowest, consisting of a slight restraint upon the freedom of action, to the highest, consisting of a long and tedious torture*". Following the report, assignment to private masters was abolished and the British Government decided to end transportation to New South Wales, preferring to send convicts sentenced to more then seven years to Port Arthur or Norfolk Island. Prisoners sentenced to fewer than seven years were punished in Britain, Gibraltar or Bermuda instead.

the FACTS!

WHILE FREE WORKERS were paid a good wage, convict workers often received their pay in rum and keep. After 1841, laws were passed that entitled freed convicts to be paid a wage. Ex-convicts were often hired to complete "piece work" tasks. A ploughman might receive 20 shillings an acre and a timber-feller might get 10 shillings per acre. Permanent workers received £25–50 annually.

ILLEGITIMATE CHILDREN were common and were often the result of relationships between female servants and their free-born masters. William Light, who planned Adelaide, was the illegitimate son of Captain Francis Light and Martina Rozells, a woman of Portuguese–Eurasian descent. William Wentworth was the illegitimate son of D'Arcy Wentworth and convict Catherine Crowley.

IN THE 1820s AND 1830s, many transported convicts farewelled their loved ones by leaving them "love tokens". Most often these were engraved coins or plaques bearing a dedication and poem or a "lament". One, inscribed to Hannah Jones from convict James Godfrey, reads: *"When in/Captivity/Time/Goeth/Very slow/But/Free as air/To roam now/Quick the/Time/Doth/Go."*

Fleeing
to freedom

Above: Irish convicts rebelled against colonial authorities at Castle Hill in 1804.

Right: An unattended row boat or cutter was a tempting sight for many convicts. Any who escaped, however, still had to brave hundreds of miles of open ocean to reach the Dutch East Indies.

the FACTS!

IN JANUARY 1798, a party was sent by Governor Hunter to the Blue Mountains to quash rumours that there were "white, civilised people" living in a spectacular city beyond the mountains. The expedition was led by an ex-convict named Wilson, who, of course, found nothing. It was hoped this would stop deluded convicts from believing this tale.

PRISONERS STOLE the *Venus* on June 17 1806. Two years later, on May 15 1808, the brig *Harrington* was also stolen from Farm Cove. The ship was later recovered in Indian waters, but the fate of the escaped convicts is unknown.

THE BRIG *CYPRUS* was seized and stolen from Macquarie Harbour by eighteen convicts on 14 August 1829. The convicts escaped, sailing the ship across the Pacific Ocean.

WILLIAM BUCKLEY'S adventure coined a popular phrase in Australian slang. People were so amazed that Buckley had managed to survive when the odds were stacked so heavily against him that when something is extremely unlikely Australians may say it has "Buckley's chance" or "Buckley's or none".

LATER IN LIFE, William Buckley went on to work as an Aboriginal interpreter.

Australia's location as an island prison — surrounded by thousands of miles of ocean or inhospitable bush populated with warrior natives — made escape a daunting prospect, but that did not stop some hopeful convicts from attempting to flee.

CONVICT BOLTERS

Escaped convicts who went bush to try to live off native animals or plunder the farms of settlers were known as "bolters" and, later, "bushrangers".

The first known bolter was a West Indian man known as "Black Caesar", who was the colony's strongest man. He was reputed to be a hard-working convict and, as such, had an enormous appetite that forced him to steal food. He escaped in May 1789 with "some provisions, an iron pot, and a soldier's musket, which he had found means to steal". David Collins' diary also mentions that he "was well known to have as small a share of veracity as honesty".

He lasted just a month before he was caught and sentenced to hang, but was later granted a reprieve and sent to work in chains growing produce on Garden Island — an extremely light sentence because most bolters and bushrangers thereafter were flogged or put to death.

ESCAPE TO CHINA

On the 21 November 1791, a party of twenty male convicts and one female convict escaped in the belief they could walk to China! They took a week's rations, bedding and tools, but it was, of course, to no avail. Aborigines attacked and wounded them and one man died of exhaustion; the rest, starving and weak, eventually straggled back to Port Jackson.

BUCKLEY'S OR NONE

In 1835, a group of nine Europeans (including Surveyor John Wedge) who were exploring near Indented Head were astonished to see a wild white man emerge from the trees. William Buckley was an escaped convict who spent 32 years living with the Wathaurong Aboriginal people after escaping from the failed British settlement at Sorrento in 1803. He had forgotten how to speak English, wore a long possum-skin cloak and carried a handful of spears.

Above: The tessellated pavements of Eaglehawk Neck.

Above: The Dog Line Monument at Eaglehawk Neck, Port Arthur, reminds today's visitors of the grim security of the penal colony, where vicious dogs and equally murderous guards patrolled.

Left: Bushranger Martin Cash.

CASH ME IF YOU CAN

Daring Irishman Martin Cash managed to escape the almost inescapable horror of Port Arthur. Along with guards, half-starved savage dogs patrolled the narrow isthmus of Eaglehawk Neck, each chained to a pole with an oil lamp dangling from it. Cash had been sentenced to seven years transportation for wounding another youth, but was later given a ticket of leave and became a free settler. Unfortunately, he was convicted for possession of stolen poultry in 1840 and sentenced to a further seven years of hard labour. Cash tried to escape twice, both times by swimming past Eaglehawk Neck. The first time he was caught but was not flogged or heavily punished, providing no deterrent to trying again. On the second occasion, in December 1842, Cash and his friends Lawrence Kavanagh and George Jones swam past Eaglehawk Neck and managed to evade the guards on East Bay Neck. The team operated as bushrangers around Hobart for several months after their escape, before being recaptured and sent to Norfolk Island as hardened criminals. Cash, however, appeared to have learnt his lesson. Unlike Kavanagh, he chose not to participate in riots that rocked Norfolk Island in July 1846 and in 1853 he was pardoned and became a free man, remaining so until his death in 1877.

THE GIRL FROM BOTANY BAY

On the 28 March 1791, Mary Bryant, who was sentenced to seven years transportation at the age of 21 for stealing a cloak, escaped with her husband William, three-year-old daughter Charlotte, baby son Emmanuel and seven other convicts. They stole the governor's six-oared cutter and rowed it, for 69 days covering over 5000 km, to Timor, where they pretended to be shipwreck survivors. Their ruse was quickly discovered when one of the men was overheard bragging about having escaped. They were arrested by Captain Edward Edwards, who had been searching for the mutineers of the *Bounty,* and were imprisoned in Batavia, where William and baby Emmanuel died of fever. Mary, along with Charlotte, was sent back to England to be tried. Charlotte died on the voyage. Back in England's Newgate Prison, Mary became famous as "the girl from Botany Bay" and was tried, officially pardoned and discharged in May 1793.

Right: Alexander Pearce was executed for killing and eating fellow escapees.

the FACTS!

ONE CONVICT TRIED to escape Port Arthur by dressing in a kangaroo skin and hopping out. He surrendered after a guard, mistaking him for a kangaroo, tried to shoot him for food!

SOMETIMES CONVICTS WHO had been issued the task of timber-getting on Sarah Island, Van Diemen's Land, absconded into the woods, trying to make the perilous journey overland to Hobart. The most famous escapee was Matthew Brady, who, with a gang of fourteen other convicts, seized a boat and rowed it out of Hell's Gates to the shores of the Derwent River. Here he terrorised settlers for two years and at one stage his gang grew to as many as 100 convicted felons — even some assigned convicts fled their masters to join his crew. He was wounded and captured near Launceston in 1826 and was hanged soon after.

ON 20 SEPTEMBER 1822, eight convicts escaped from Macquarie Harbour in Van Diemen's Land, but things quickly turned bad — facing starvation, Alexander Pearce (below) turned cannibal and ate his fellow escapees! He confessed to this crime when caught, but was not believed. Pearce escaped again in 1823, this time accompanied by an unfortunate convict named Thomas Cox. When Pearce discovered Cox could not swim a river to escape, he killed and ate Cox too. He was caught with human flesh in his pocket and was condemned to death and executed in Hobart on 19 July 1824.

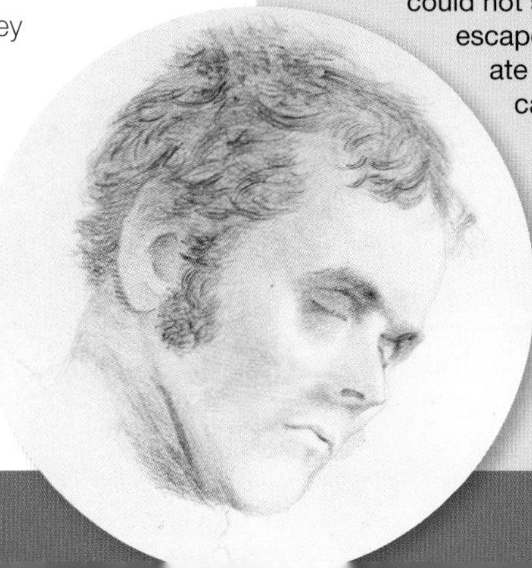

Very important people

Many people, living in many different colonies, contributed to the success of Australia; however, some made an indelible mark on the nation's history for their enterprise, their vision or their notoriety.

Above: **Lands Commissioner and Premier John Robertson became the hero of the ordinary man for opening the land to free selection.**

GOVERNOR SIR RICHARD BOURKE

Dublin-born Richard Bourke (right) arrived in Sydney on 3 December 1831 to take up the post of governor. Over the next six years he proved himself a far-sighted governor for the people, implementing (against the wishes of the exclusives) the right to trial by civil jury for criminal cases, and requiring squatters to pay an annual licence to lease land. He also moved a bill that stopped magistrates from sentencing convicts to harsher punishments than were given to other perpetrators, which led to one of his main critics, the *Sydney Morning Herald,* calling the bill Bourke's "soothing system for convicts". During his time as governor he also made unsuccessful proposals for government-funded schools and elective representation. When he departed the colony in 1837, so great was public admiration for Bourke that crowds of people gathered and sent him off with resounding ovation.

MACARTHUR & HIS MERINOS

In 1790, John Macarthur (below), a Lieutenant of the New South Wales Corps, arrived in the Sydney colony with his wife Elizabeth (bottom) and baby son Edward. He went on to become one of Australia's wealthiest settlers. The Macarthurs were originally granted 41 ha in Parramatta, which they named Elizabeth Farm. The famous Elizabeth House (Australia's oldest building) still stands on the spot today. In 1797, Macarthur imported four merino ewes and two rams from South Africa and began producing wool, later establishing another estate at Cowpastures (now Camden) in 1805. By 1811, Australia's first large shipment of wool was sent to England and by 1825 the colony had exported 146,800 kg of wool to Britain, making Australia the third-largest wool supplier to Britain at the time.

Macarthur became an important trader and a very powerful man but records suggest that he was not particularly well liked, although his more humble wife, Elizabeth, was well respected.

the FACTS!

GOVERNOR ARTHUR PHILLIP ruled New South Wales from 1788–1792, followed by the New South Wales Corps (under the command of Grose and Paterson) from 1792–1795. In 1795, Governor John Hunter resumed control until 1800. Phillip Gidley King then governed from 1800–1806, followed by the (later deposed) William Bligh from 1806–1808. Governor Macquarie spent the longest time as governor, from 1810–1822. He was succeeded by Governors Thomas Brisbane, Ralph Darling and Richard Bourke.

JOHN MACARTHUR was widely regarded as an ambitious, stubborn and haughty bully. His father had owned a lucrative drapery in Plymouth, so John's many enemies nicknamed him "Jack Boddice, a military stay-makers apprentice". Macarthur made many enemies.

ONE OF THE SONS of John and Elizabeth Macarthur had a bodyguard made up of Aborigines who were well dressed and rode around with him on horseback.

SETTLEMENT WOULD HAVE been difficult without explorers such as Sir Thomas Mitchell, Charles Sturt and Ludwig Liechhardt paving the way.

SIR GEORGE ARTHUR

George Arthur (right), the fifth governor of Van Diemen's Land, took command in 1824. He was one of the harshest and most hated colonial administrators, but nevertheless played an important part in Tasmania's governance. He established the Port Arthur prison and Port Puer "model" prison for boys and was responsible for Tasmania's devastating policy of segregation, which lead to the displacement of Tasmanian Aborigines.

SIR JOHN ROBERTSON

One of Australia's least-likely politicians, former squatter and self-confessed "bushman" John Robertson, played a major role in land law reform. Although born in Bow, England, he identified with the colony-born "cornstalks" and insisted that although "an English infant … as a man I am an Australian!" In the political landscape of the 1850s, Robertson's electoral platform was vote by secret ballot, electoral districts based on population, national education, free trade, and free selection of Crown Lands before survey. His land bills allowed poor selectors a chance at land ownership.

GOVERNOR LACHLAN MACQUARIE

Governor Macquarie (bottom right) was born in Scotland and was a highly regarded commander of the 73rd Regiment before he served as governor of New South Wales from 1810–1822. During his tenure, the convict population increased rapidly as settlers demanded convict labour. Macquarie was a humane man who tried to fairly distribute prisoners while still maintaining pubic works. He had grand visions for the colony and as soon as he arrived he set about making it more civilised by banning pigs from being allowed to run in the streets, shoring up falling down roads and buildings, insisting that houses must be numbered and forbidding washing clothing in the Tank Stream, which was the colony's water supply.

Macquarie instigated many of Sydney's fine constructions and his legacy remains in some of Sydney's gracious heritage buildings. A road was built to Parramatta, a lighthouse erected at South Head, and factories, stables and barracks were constructed. In 1819, with settlers not providing enough work for convicts, Macquarie built the first convict barracks and reinstituted government farms. The female factory at Parramatta was also rebuilt by Macquarie, who deemed it "particularly Necessary for keeping those Depraved Females at Work within Walls, so as in some Degree to be a Check upon their Immoralities and disorderly Vicious Habits".

Macquarie treated convicts and free settlers with equality and from 1817–1821 many people condemned him for being too lenient. Over his term, Macquarie freed 300 convicts on pardons and granted 1365 conditional pardons. During his governance, 20–25% of the prisoners arriving in Sydney were granted tickets of leave almost immediately. In 1819, JT Bigge was sent to investigate Macquarie's lenient management of the colony. Macquarie refused to believe that under his command transportation had lost its deterrent, but Bigge criticised Macquarie for his tendency to treat ex-convicts as equals. Bigge found out that 44 convicts who were instructed to cut grass to feed the colony's horses and cattle were entitled to sell any excess grass themselves once they had filled their quota — according to Bigge, this kind of enterprise made transportation less of a deterrent for convicts. By 1821, Macquarie was ill and tired of the conjecture over his command of the colony. He resigned and returned to England in 1822, before Bigge's "vile document" (as he later called Bigge's report) was published.

the FACTS!

JOHN ROBERTSON had been born with a cleft palate, which affected his speech, making him the brunt of jokes from some detractors.

MINING SURVEYOR John Busby provided Sydney with its first water supply by running a tunnel from today's Centennial Park to Hyde Park and a standpipe in the city.

IN 1814, Macquarie initiated a school for Aboriginal children, called the "Native Institution". It aimed to teach the children to read and write English and to learn mechanics, labouring, sewing and knitting.

ELIZABETH MACQUARIE, the wife of Governor Macquarie, established the Female Orphan School in Parramatta in 1813. The school was expanded and boys admitted after 1850.

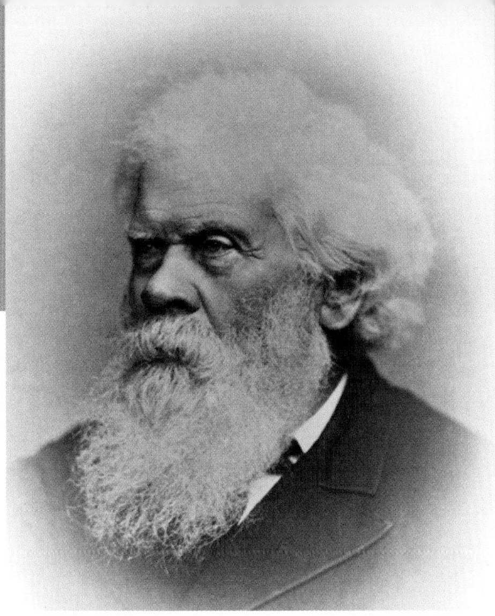

the FACTS!

PHILANTHROPIST George Fife Angas (above) migrated to South Australia in 1851. Before then, as the England-based Chairman of the South Australian Company, he had been instrumental in helping German Lutherans, fleeing religious persecution, migrate to South Australia from 1838. When he arrived in Australia in 1851 he immediately entered the Legislative Council, holding the seat of Barossa until 1866. Angus also established several early Australian banks.

DAVID SYME arrived in Australia to try his hand at digging for gold in 1852, but went on to be one of Australia's earliest media magnates. In 1856, he took over *The Age* newspaper with the help of his brother Ebenezer. Syme ran the paper for 49 years after his brother died in 1859. He became one of the colony's most powerful and well respected men. Journalists such as David Syme and William Wentworth had enormous influence on policy decisions to open the land to selectors and to allow emancipists to sit on legislative councils.

SIR HENRY PARKES

Henry Parkes (above) was not born in the colony but migrated to New South Wales in 1839. At first, he found life extremely difficult, originally working as a customs officer before later setting up an import business. Parkes later became a journalist and social reformer who established the *Empire* newspaper and quickly became active in the media. In 1854, he entered politics and he was elected to the New South Wales Legislative Assembly in 1856. Parkes remained an active politician until 1895 and twice served as premier of New South Wales. He later became Sir Henry Parkes and was one of the most outspoken advocates for Federation. Given his political history and his renown as a powerful orator, his suggestion that a convention be held to discuss Federation and the drawing up of a federal constitution were adopted. Unfortunately, Sir Henry Parkes never lived to see his dream come to fruition. He died in 1896, five years before Federation was achieved for the new nation.

THE CATTLE KING

Sir Sidney Kidman, the "Cattle King", was one of Australia's most successful graziers — at one time owning more land than anyone in Australia. He worked as a stockman in New South Wales from the age of thirteen until his entrepreneurial streak led him to set himself up as a butcher, and then as a trader. By the 1880s, he and his brother ran a coach business through South Australia, New South Wales and Queensland. Using the money they earned, they purchased cattle stations between Queensland and Adelaide.

THE HENTY FAMILY

Wealthy Thomas Henty, along with his wife, seven sons and one daughter, first arrived to seek his fortune in Western Australia in 1829 where the family was granted 84,413 acres around Swan River. Finding it unsuitable they sought to exchange their untenable land for fewer acres in Van Diemen's Land, but their request was denied, leading to the family squatting and profiting from whaling and wool at Portland Bay. On Thomas's death in Launceston in 1839, his sons went on to become successful squatters, merchants and politicians.

THE ENDURING DURACKS

The Duracks formed a pioneering dynasty after Michael and Jeremiah arrived in the country from Ireland in 1840 and 1853. Michael's sons Patrick and Michael, went on to establish large properties such as Thylungra and Kyabra stations in south-western Queensland. Upon hearing of excellent grazing country in the Western Australian Kimberley region, Patrick Durack later drove 7000 cattle and 200 horses more than 4800 km to the region — a journey which took 2.5 years and was at the time the longest overlanding effort by Australian drovers. Patrick Durack's sons later established Argyle Downs station in the Kimberley and other properties in the Ord Basin. The Duracks also founded the firm Conner, Doherty and Durack Ltd, which was instrumental to Australia's beef export trade. Michael Durack later entered politics and his daughter Mary (left) became a popular author who wrote of her life on Argyle Downs station in her famous work *Kings in Grass Castles*.

The rush for gold

Above: Samuel Thomas Gill's painting depicts the rush to the Ballarat goldfields in 1854.

From 1851, the lure of gold drew many millions of "diggers" to Australia. Very few of them made the fortune they desired, but after the gold rush few of them left. Most stayed on to see what other rewards the new country had to offer.

BATHURST WAS THE SITE of the first gold discovery in February 1851 and by May of the same year as many as 1000 "diggers", as the fortune hunters were known, had set themselves up in bark "humpies" along Lewis Ponds Creek. The shanty gold town was named Ophir (a biblical name for a "golden city") by Edward Hargraves, who had first discovered gold. More gold was soon discovered at Ballarat, Castlemaine and Bendigo, sparking a rush to the goldfields. Fortune hunters from around the globe and across the country hurried to the goldfields, mostly travelling alone and leaving their families at home, on their properties or in the cities. "Every man and boy who is able to lift a shovel is off, or going off, to the diggings," wrote one English ship's captain in 1851.

Most diggers walked hundreds of kilometres to try their luck, but wealthier prospectors rode horses or travelled by horse-drawn coach or cart. Some pushed their meagre possessions (including a pick, a shovel and a panning dish) in a wheelbarrow, others swung a swag over their shoulders. Horses could be a liability because there were no blacksmiths on the goldfields and bushrangers often attacked parties on horseback and stole their mounts. Squatters also cursed the goldrush because it meant they had to pay labourers more to stop them from leaving to seek their fortune.

A LIVING ON THE DIGGINGS

Making a fortune was far from easy. Miners worked six days a week, digging a deep shaft, sifting mud and soil in a cradle and then panning the specks of dirt, rock and (hopefully!) gold, in water. When prospectors found gold (and many did not), it was sold to brokers working for city banks or to private goldfield-based buyers, who had a reputation for being unscrupulous. Some grew extremely long fingernails that they could scrape through the gold and then run through their hair, later collecting the precious gold from their scalps! Others tampered with their scales so that gold measured light and they could pay less for it. However, some diggers got their own back by plating a false nugget of lead or copper with a thin layer of gold. Many miners could not be bothered dealing with dishonest buyers, so they paid shopkeepers in gold and let the shopkeeper trade the precious metal instead. Bushrangers were also hungry for gold, so gold escorts were set up to carry gold to the cities. Troopers rode with the gold and charged a commission of 1% of the gold's worth to keep it safe. The first gold escort was in 1851, travelling from Ballarat to Geelong.

the FACTS!

THE DISCOVERY of gold saw a massive influx in immigration from 1851–1857. In three years (1851–1854), the population of Ballarat jumped from 4000 to 47,000.

FREEMAN COBB established the first coach service to the goldfields in 1854 and later formed the famous Cobb & Co (below). The coaches carried mail, passengers and gold to and from Melbourne and the goldfields. When the going got tough on the boggy dirt roads, passengers had to push!

"YOU COULD SEE the gold shining in the heaps of dirt and every man sat on his heap all night with a pistol" wrote one reporter about Ballarat.

NOT EVERYONE made their fortune on the goldfields. Glamorous magicians, chorus girls, dancers and actors all grew rich providing entertainment for miners. Local halls held balls and performed theatre. One performer, Lola Montez, even horse-whipped a newspaper editor for writing that her show was indecent!

Above: The goldfields were multicultural, but not everyone got along as well as these three men in Joseph Colin Francis's painting *A game of euchre.*

Life on the goldfields

Most diggers brought strips of canvas with them to fashion into tents — sometimes by just draping the strip over a tree branch. Others built bark huts or, if they had decided to stay for a while, wattle-and-daub or rough wooden slab huts.

the FACTS!

MOST MINERS only washed once a week. In fact, most people in the 1800s only bathed on Sundays. Clothes were mostly washed every few weeks but some miners just hung them over a branch and beat the dust and dirt out with a stick! Later, wealthier miners could afford to use laundries, which were usually run by Chinese immigrants.

MANY MINERS WERE illiterate and paid clerks to write letters home to their loved ones or to read letters for them. Letters were sent off with the newly invented penny stamp and travelled by Royal Mail coach. In 1856, steamships began to carry mail back to England, allowing British miners to send letters home. Huge queues formed outside the makeshift post office when the mail coach was due.

THERE WAS no way of refrigerating meat, but some travelling butchers often sold rancid mutton from the back of a butcher's wagon (below). Miners were suspicious of tinned meat, which was known as "tinned dog" in some places.

DANGEROUS PAINKILLERS such as morphine and opium could even be bought from an apothecary.

BARBERS were often also employed as makeshift dentists and pulled teeth as well as cutting hair!

HOME AND HEALTH

Housing was very rough! A fireplace at one end of a tent or hut kept the digger's belongings dry, but there was little security. After a while, some diggers built huts from flattened ironbark stretched over a frame of saplings and tree branches and sometimes lined with canvas. Window panes were left empty or covered with timber shutters to keep out dust, insects and poisonous snakes and spiders.

Medical treatment was not available, so if diggers became ill they tried to cure their ills with sometimes suspicious "potions" from an apothecary (untrained pharmacist). The crowded goldfields were also a hotbed for contagious diseases such as cholera and typhoid, which could quickly kill malnourished miners. Mining accidents, fires, and horse and cart accidents were also common causes of injury or death.

FASHIONS ON THE FIELD

European clothing was unsuitable for the heat and hard work of the goldfields so men wore heavy twill trousers or water-repellent moleskins and shirts of serge. A knotted handkerchief was used to wipe away sweat and wide-brimmed hats woven from cabbage-tree palms or felt were also worn. Chinese miners wore loose, buttoned jackets, trousers and conical hats woven from straw and varnished to keep out the rain. Wealthy "gentlemen" wore the three-piece trouser, waistcoat and jacket favoured in the cities with a pocket watch as a sign of their wealth.

DAMPER AND DRINK

Shops on the goldfields at first were little more than folding tables filled with wares, but soon permanent storekeepers moved in. Because many wheat and crop farmers had left to try their luck prospecting, prices for flour and vegetables skyrocketed. Storekeepers took advantage and charged up to twelve times the usual price, so most diggers existed on a simple diet of damper, meat and tea. Luxuries were tobacco, pickled fruit and vegetables, tinned sardines, cookware and clothing. Soon, "cook-shops" sprang up to provide soup, pies and stews for the hungry miners. Cook-shops were often run by Chinese immigrants and many became far more lucrative than gold mining.

The most common drink was strong, black billy tea. Water was often dirty, so boiling it with tea killed diseases and masked the taste. Alcohol was illegal at first but women's skirts were perfect for hiding a small cask and some women ran a small pipe out from a pocket to serve rum to miners for a price. Some shopkeepers also paid miners their change in alcohol.

Right: **Hawkers (travelling salesmen) travelled from tent to tent selling pies and pastries.**

Eureka stockade

Above: The Eureka Centre stands on the original site of the uprising on Eureka Street in East Ballarat.

Left: The Eureka Stockade — police outnumbered the miners two to one.

Colonial governments tried to establish law and order on the goldfields by banning alcohol, introducing gold mining licences, appointing a gold commissioner and sending police and troopers to the goldfields, but riots and fights continued.

NATIVE POLICE FORCE

Theft, alcoholism and fights were common and a police force to keep the violence and lawlessness in check was required. The first policemen on the goldfields were the Native Police Corps, a crack team of Aboriginal trackers who were excellent riders and hoped to be able to track down criminals and bushrangers quickly. Miners called them "Joes", after their founder, Governor Joseph La Trobe. They were very good at their jobs but other Aborigines and Europeans began to resent them and they were disbanded in 1853.

A LICENCE TO REBEL

The colonies still needed farmers and the government hoped that by charging a licence fee some of the less successful diggers would return to farming. Licences cost approximately 30 shillings (around $150) a month and diggers had to have their licence on them at all times, even when digging in mud or water that could ruin the paper licences. If miners couldn't immediately produce a licence they were dragged off to prison or chained up by the police. Consequently the diggers had no respect for the police and began to rebel.

A VOTE FOR THE EVERYDAY MAN

Trouble on the goldfields began in October 1854, when miner James Scobie was killed in a fight outside Bentley's Hotel, Ballarat. His friends believed hotel owner, James Bentley, was the killer and marched on the hotel, burning it down. Bentley was later found guilty of manslaughter and some miners were imprisoned for burning down the hotel. After the trial, citizens formed the Ballarat Reform League, which demanded the release of the convicted miners, the abolition of licence fees and a vote. Only landowners and squatters had the right to vote, but the diggers argued that they paid more for their licences than the squatters did for their leases, so the licences were effectively a land tax that should entitle them to a vote. However, Governor Hotham refused to meet their demands, causing many diggers to publicly burn their licences and defiantly wave the Southern Cross flag.

On 29 November, after another licence hunt, fights broke out between troops and miners. The following day, Irishmen Peter Lalor (below right) addressed miners on Bakery Hill, urging them to build a stockade, swear an oath to "stand by each other" and fight the troops. By 2 December the stockade had been built. Unfortunately for the miners, the soldiers attacked at 4.45 am on Sunday 3 December, when many miners had left the stockade, believing they wouldn't be attacked on the holy day. The miners were outnumbered two to one and many were killed. Peter Lalor escaped with a wounded arm, which was later amputated, and the bloodied Southern Cross was torn down. Although the Eureka uprising was put down, it did bring about a change to the laws.

the FACTS!

VICTORIA HAD ONLY JUST become a colony, so Governor La Trobe had just 44 soldiers and 40 policemen available to him in 1851— and all but two of his policemen were intent on quitting to seek their fortune!

MANY RACIST MINERS persecuted Chinese diggers, who were unfairly subject to special taxes and whose numbers were eventually restricted by the Victorian government. In 1857, 120 miners attacked the Chinese camp in the Ovens Valley and burnt their tents and temples. More than 2400 Chinese were killed, most drowning in the river as they hurried to escape the racist mob. From 1860–1861, the violence escalated and bloody attacks killed more Chinese miners at Lambing Flat, the present site of Young, New South Wales.

EVENTUALLY, PETER LALOR was not only allowed to vote but was elected to Legislative Council, representing the goldfields district for more than thirty years!

Above: Miners waved flags bearing the Southern Cross.

Above: Staking a claim.

On our selection — "cockatoo" farmers

After the gold rush, unsuccessful prospectors began to resent the squatters' monopoly of the land. By the end of the 1850s, they cried for the government to "unlock the land".

IN 1861, *THE CROWN LANDS ACT* allowed anyone to take up "selections" from 4–320 acres for just £1 per acre, on the condition that they paid a 25% deposit upfront and lived on the land for three years with the intention of farming crops. This opened up the bush to the selectors, but caused ongoing struggles with the squatters, who had leased the best runs for years and were reluctant to hand over parts of their properties.

A CORNSTALK'S DREAM

Squatters often employed tricks to keep their land, such as placing "dummy" selectors in temporary huts on the land, sending their servants out to sleep in huts on the selections or buying up the only watered land themselves, leaving selectors with the driest plots. Some squatters even sent themselves bankrupt by borrowing a lot of money to buy their runs in their own name and the names of family members.

However, owning the land was a dream come true for the quietly ambitious selectors who looked upon their plot with great optimism at first. Famous author Steele Rudd (Arthur Hoey Davis) described the joy of a man taking up a selection:

> *You'll ride all over it filled with the proud spirit of ownership. Every inch of it and everything on it will be yours—the growing timber; the logs and firewood lying about; hundreds of fencing-posts that some poor cove's split and had to abandon; the old sheepyard and shepherd's hut that were erected by someone who went insolvent; even the wild flowers and darn stones'll be yours! How you'll admire it all!*

SUBSISTENCE EXISTENCE

Life for a selector was extremely hard. Most selectors did not have enough capital to make the small selection a viable enterprise, instead clinging to the hope that they could, over the years, breed enough animals or grow enough crops to pay back what they owed to the local storeowner or private lenders (who charged exorbitant interest rates, sometimes as high as 35%). Often, by the time the free selectors had scratched together their first crop, they owed all the profit to local businesses.

the FACTS!

SELECTORS WERE KNOWN as "cockies" because they were often extremely poor and "pecked up the grains of a living", just like a cockatoo. Later, when sugar cane farming became a booming industry in Queensland's north, "cane cockies" as they were known, became quite wealthy.

A POPULAR BALLAD following the *Land Act* went: *Come all of you Cornstalks, the victory's won/John Robertson's triumphed, the lean days are gone/No more through the bush we'll go humping the drum/For the Land Bill has passed and the good times have come/No more through the bush with our swags need we roam/ For to ask of the squatters to give us a home/Now the land is unfettered and we may reside/In a place of our own by the clear waterside/We will sow our own garden and till our own field/ And eat of the fruits that our labour doth yield/And be independent, a right long denied/By those who have ruled us and robbed us beside.*

Right: Arthur Hoey Davis, better known as Steele Rudd, grew up on a poor selection, inspiring Dad & Dave.

Below: A stage show of the popular *On Our Selection*, written by Steele Rudd.

Above: Selectors constructed slab huts in much the same away as the early squatters until corrugated iron and mill-sawn timber made it easier to create housing.

STOREKEEPERS OFTEN BARTERED the produce brought in by selectors against cash loans, deducting up to 70% of the value; others allowed selectors to run up huge accounts. Steele Rudd recounts that when his father's first harvest of corn was sold by the shopkeeper for £12, as much as £9 was deducted to pay store bills. He writes that his father *"looked sick … went home and sat on a block and stared into the fire"*. Most struggled to feed and clothe their families, although some of those lucky enough to obtain fertile land around the Darling Downs or the Murray River made a comfortable living. Close to the coast, where poor soils made crop farming difficult, dairy farming became the selector's salvation.

A FAMILY AFFAIR

Compared to the squatters, selectors were trying to eke out a living on very small properties. Also, most of the selectors had their wives and children with them, while the squatters left their families in the cities. Selectors could not afford to pay for labour, so they usually had large families to help them work on the land. Some men, unable to earn enough from their struggling harvest, were forced to also take up part-time work, leaving their families to do the bulk of the farm work. Poet Henry Lawson grew up on a selection near Gulgong, New South Wales, and was "kicked out of bed at four in the morning to milk cows and ... kicked right through the day till nine and ten o'clock at night doing this, that and everything." Because he was needed on the selection, he attended school for just three years and was consequently a very poor speller. He wrote of the despair the selectors faced and said, "Saw selectors slaving their lives away in dusty holes amongst the barren ridges: saw one or two carried home, in the end, on a sheet of bark; the old men worked till they died".

DREAMS TO DUST

Despite the great hope that the land laws would give small crop farmers a greater opportunity for wealth, few of the selectors were successful. Those that did manage to make a living from the soil contributed much to the success of Australia's small rural communities and towns, but many of the free selectors ended up in debt and were forced off the land they had fought so long and hard to obtain. Of the 450,000 acres of selections taken up in Victoria's Gippsland Hills, more than half had been denuded and abandoned by the end of the 19th century. Eventually it became clear that the idea of the "little man" being able to make a profitable living on a small block was impractical for most of the Australian landscape. Selectors, worn out with trying, abandoned their life's dream and flocked to the already crowded cities, where most of Australia's population is still gathered today.

Right: Hopeful selectors travelled to their plot of land with very little but their optimism about finally being able to make their own fortune.

the FACTS!

SELECTORS OFTEN KEPT chickens and cows, but not everyone could afford such luxuries. Some selectors were so poor they couldn't even afford tea leaves. Steele Rudd describes how his parents used burnt bread and hot water as a tea substitute. Meat was salted to make it last longer or was kept in a "Coolgardie safe", a wooden frame covered in wet hessian. The meat inside was kept cool and was out of the reach of flies as the water in the hessian evaporated. Golden syrup (known as "Cocky's joy") was used to sweeten tea and spread on damper.

BY THE 1880S, plagues of rabbits destroyed many selectors' last hopes of remaining on the land, but at least they provided welcome meat for starving families.

SELECTORS' HUTS SMELLED bad because dishwater, bath water and chamber pots were emptied close to the house, coupled with the smell of burning mutton-fat candles, and cow manure, which was thrown on the fire at night to help keep the mosquitoes away.

Above: Pioneers had to milk their own livestock and make their own butter and cheese.

Pioneering women

A woman's work in the bush was never done. Most women worked from daylight to dusk, washing, tending the vegetable patch, keeping cows, chicken and sheep, baking bread, churning butter and setting cheese, as well as looking after their children and preparing and cooking meals for the family.

WOMEN OFTEN HAD to keep the station or selection running while their husbands were away droving stock to market or attending to business in the cities. Pioneering women lived a lonely, isolated existence and droughts, fires, floods, snakes and unassisted childbirth were just some of the trials and tribulations faced. Usually the nearest homestead was hundreds of kilometres away, so there was very little company for women. Respectable ladies would never be seen in a sly grog shop so opportunities to socialise were few. Many women feared rape or attack from the swagmen or itinerants that travelled the outback seeking work. One pioneering woman, Emma Withnell, was left alone with her ten children on their station near Dampier, Western Australia for extended periods while her husband was working as a pearler. Her memoirs record how she one day became so afraid that someone was outside that she fired off a shot from a shotgun, only to later realise she had shot at her own hat and dress hanging on the line!

Above: Washing was done by hand.

the FACTS!

CLOTHES WERE BOILED in a copper, then dragged into a wash tub where they were pounded with a "wash dolly" (a wooden paddle) or a "posser" (a plunger) before being hand-wrung or "mangled".

WOMEN MOSTLY cooked on open fires until the 1860s when most people owned wood stoves.

BUTTER COULD TAKE up to 2.5 hours to make by hand-churning cream that was filtered off the top of cow's milk.

IRONING WAS HOT and heavy work as hot metal irons heated on the stove were used.

WOMEN EVEN HAD TO make their own soap by boiling down animal fat, blending it with caustic soda and hardening it in cut-down kerosene tins.

SOME GERMAN WOMEN living around Hahndorf in South Australia even sheared sheep! They used to tie a string around their big toe and use the length to tie the sheep's legs. Around 30 sheep a day were shorn by the stoic women.

THERE WAS NO contraception, so women often had as many as seventeen children, some of whom died as infants or as young children in the tough conditions. Because of the vast distances, a midwife rarely made it in time to attend pregnant women, so they often gave birth alone, attended by their family.
In Australia in the 1820s, one in every ten children died before their first birthday.

THROUGH DROUGHT, FLOOD AND FIRE

Martha Cox, who farmed in western New South Wales in the early 1870s, recounted her experience of drought in her memoir. "Day by day the water went lower in the tank … if rain did not come soon it meant ruin for there was no chance of shifting the poor sheep. Every green thing disappeared and only the dry grass seed, which the sheep licked up, stood between them and starvation … Our great drawback was lack of vegetables because our tank water was too precious to use on a vegetable garden." Later, Martha and her husband moved to Wagga Wagga and Martha took over running the station when her husband died. A bushfire laid to waste 1400 sheep and burnt down her home, but Martha and her farmhands carried on, rebuilding the home and station. Other famous pioneer women were Jeannie Gun (of *We of the Never Never* fame), Miles Franklin, Eliza Fraser, Georgiana Molloy and Georgiana McRae.

Outback governesses

The Female Middle Class Emigration Society was established in 1862 to attract educated governesses to the colonies. Many lived difficult and boring lives in the outback.

FORMIDABLE FEMINISTS

Australia's determined female settlers did not just have to battle the bush, they also had to fight for their rights in a society that was largely male-dominated. Until the late 1800s, women in Australia had no equality. Australian women were not entitled to vote until 1902, after Federation (although South Australian women received a vote earlier).

Until the 1870s, women were unable to own property unless they were single, because after marriage all of a woman's personal property belonged to her husband. Women were also unable to become lawyers or doctors, or study at university until the late 1880s. In the colony of New South Wales, women were also unable to take up land grants; although, if their father's salary was too meagre to support them, young single women were able to apply for a land grant as part of their marriage dowry. This was the government's way of providing an incentive for men and women to marry.

Eliza Walsh, who arrived in Sydney in 1819, helped change the rules of land ownership by enabling women to be granted land independently. She initially bought a small piece of land when she arrived in 1819, and applied to Governor Macquarie for more in 1820, stating that she had bought cattle worth £1000 and would buy another £1000 worth of stock were she granted more land. Her request was denied because the governor wrote that it was not fitting to "give Grants of lands to Ladies".

Eliza immediately wrote to the English secretary of state, complaining, "a Lady is able to conduct a Farm as well as a Gentleman". The secretary of state wrote back to Governor Macquarie, "I am not aware of any reason why females, who are unmarried, should be secluded from holding Lands in the Colony". Eventually, nine years later, Eliza Walsh was granted land at Paterson River in the Hunter Valley of New South Wales.

A FEMALE FIRST

One of the most important women in Australian history was journalist and novelist Catherine Spence (below right). She was just fourteen when she arrived in Adelaide in 1839. She went on to be the first woman to write a novel about life in Australia, and to become Australia's first female political candidate. Like Caroline Chisholm, Catherine Spence was also a social reformer who campaigned to help orphaned or poverty-stricken women and children and to improve education. She was a staunch campaigner for a more democratic electoral system, championing women's right to vote. Thanks in part to her efforts, and those of the Women's Suffrage League and the Women's Christian Temperance Union, in 1894 South Australia became the first place in Australia where women could vote. In 1897, when she stood (unsuccessfully) for the federal convention, Catherine Spence became the first female political candidate in Australian history.

the FACTS!

AGNES BUNTINE was a heroine of the gold rush of the 1850s. As tough as any man, Agnes was the first known female bullock driver and once rescued a young girl by bullock-whipping the girl's attackers. Agnes also worked as a gold escort. William Howitt wrote of her "*... she drove down to Melbourne with the Gold Escort with a pair of pistols in her belt ... and told the troopers with the Escort she would protect them in case of attack from bushrangers*".

LOUSIA LAWSON, mother of poet Henry Lawson, was a true pioneering feminist. She lived in a bark hut on the goldfields before moving to a property near Mudgee, New South Wales. In 1883, she moved to Sydney and established Australia's first feminist magazine *The Dawn*. The journal gave fashion tips and advice but also advocated the right to vote and commented on suffragette activity around the world.

CONSTANCE STONE was the first Australian-born female doctor, but because female medical students were not allowed in Australia until the late 1800s, she had to study overseas.

EVEN NURSING was not seen as a respectable occupation for a middle-class woman.

Transport
& technology

At first, communication between the colonies was sporadic because written messages had to be carried by boat or on foot. Horses and bullocks were scarce — only rich settlers could afford them in the early days of settlement — so convicts were used to tow carts and pull ploughs. Later, railways, paddlesteamers and telegraph lines made life easier.

LONG TRAINS RUNNING

Between 1820 and 1850, communication increased and transport became faster. When Sydney's first railway was opened in 1855, goods were able to be more easily transported from the wharves to those wishing to sell the wares. By 1869, a southern line was opened to Goulburn, making trade easier and a western line was put through to Bathurst in 1876. Albury was accessible by rail from Sydney from 1881 and a bridge over the Murray River at Albury linked the Victorian rail system with Sydney. Newcastle and Sydney conducted trade by sea until 1889, when a railway bridge over the Hawkesbury River was constructed. Finally, the rail system linked Brisbane with Adelaide and the capital cities of the other States.

A LINK DOWN THE LINE

In the 1840s, the invention of the electric telegraph had a profound effect on communication around the world. As telegraph lines began to link major cities to one another, messages could be quickly relayed in morse code. London-born astronomer Charles Todd arrived in South Australia in 1855 and began to supervise the establishment of Australia's first telegraph line. By 1856, suburban telegraph lines were established and by 1858, a telegraph line linked Adelaide and Melbourne. In 1877, it stretched from Adelaide to Perth. In 1870, Todd managed to persuade governments and investors to finance the hefty £480,000 required to build the overland Telegraph Line across 3200 km of inhospitable, arid country to connect Adelaide and the rest of Australia, through Darwin, with England. It took two years (1870–1872) to complete and ran from Port Augusta to Darwin; an undersea cable connected it to Indonesia and on to London. Finally, Australia had a fast and reliable connection with Europe and the outside world, which also dramatically reduced the amount of time it took to get a message across the continent. Further communication services followed, with the first telephone exchange beginning operations in Melbourne in 1880. At that time, it had just 44 subscribers, which were listed in Australia's first ever printed telephone directory.

the FACTS!

HORSES WERE SCARCE at first. Even by 1810, there were only 1134 horses in the colony.

BULLOCKS were rarely used to pull carts until the 1820s.

FREEMAN COBB established the first Cobb & Co coach run to Bendigo during the gold rush, changing horses every 16 km. By the 1860s, the company was one of the most successful in Australia.

GOODS HAD TO BE unloaded and reloaded onto different trains at the State border because each State had a different gauge (thickness) of railway track. Mainland interstate is now standardised, but gauge widths still vary within States.

FERRIES LINKED SUBURBS such as Manly, Mosman and Cremorne with central Sydney, and Circular Quay was the main centre for passenger travel, leaving cargo ships to dock at Darling Harbour.

THE ARRIVAL of the "automobile" (below) in the 1900s revolutionised Australian transport, allowing goods to be quickly transported.

Right: The Overland Telegraph team of (from left to right) JAG Little, Robert Patterson, Charles Todd and WW Mitchell.

Above, left to right: The Old Ghan Railway, South Australia; The invention of farm machinery revolutionised agriculture; Historic Trebonne Post Office. Stamps were invented in Australia to make postage easier for those in remote areas.

REVOLUTIONARY ADVANCES

Newly invented farm machinery began to make life easier for settlers in the 1800s. In 1843, farmer John Ridley invented a machine known as a "stripper", which allowed grain to be easily plucked from standing wheat. The machine did the same amount of work it would take ten men to do by hand and dramatically reduced harvesting costs per acre. His design was based on a model harvester created by John Bull two months earlier. Later, in 1876, South Australian Robert Bowyer Smith and his eleven-year-old brother Clarence Herbert conceived the idea for the stump-jump plough, which could dig up the otherwise untillable mallee soil without being wrecked on tree roots or stumps. In the early 1880s an Irishman named Mullen developed the mallee-roller to level scrub. Clearing scrub in this way became known as "Mullenising". While many worked to combine technologies into a harvester, the first commercially available combine harvester was designed by Hugh Victor McKay and constructed by McCalman, Garde & Co in 1885.

Australia is a dry continent but it was only in the late 1880s that the Chaffey brothers, George and William, pioneered irrigation, pumping water from the Murray River at Renmark, South Australia, and Mildura, Victoria. Some reports believe irrigation may also have been used to grow hops at Redlands as early as 1843, but this is unconfirmed.

Above: Paddlesteamers plied the Murray.

Below: Puffing Billy, which still runs in the Dandenong Ranges, is Victoria's oldest steam locomotive.

FULL STEAM AHEAD

In the 1800s, the invention of the steam engine had a major influence on Australia. Skilled workers rushed to New South Wales after the first steam engine arrived in 1815. Within 45 years, steam engines, either imported or built in the colony, were powering sugar refineries, meat canning factories and iron and copper-smelting industries, as well as fuelling ships and making gas.

As industries grew, more ships were required for trade, both between the colonies and to export goods overseas. The first shipyard opened in 1797 at the Rocks in Sydney, and the following year the first private shipyard opened. By 1812 Van Diemen's Land had its own shipyard and others followed in Western Australia in 1835, South Australia in 1837, Melbourne in 1839 and Moreton Bay in 1849. Ships built in the colony were soon transporting goods throughout the Pacific and Australia's shipyards became bustling centres of industry.

the **FACTS**!

THE RACK mechanical wool press was invented in Melbourne in 1865. Two years later, the first mechanical shearing machine was patented by JAB Higham.

FENCING WIRE was introduced in the 1880s — before then pastoralists had to laboriously build stone or wooden fences or pay shepherds to control flocks. Fencing paddocks was cheaper than employing shepherds so boundary riders replaced shepherds on stations.

ARTESIAN WATER was first found in 1878 at Kallara Station near Bourke, NSW. Artesian bores enabled settlement away from rivers and into western Queensland and New South Wales. The first bore was sunk in Queensland in 1887.

TECHNOLOGICAL developments from 1880 to 1900, such as the centrifugal cream separator, refrigeration, pasteurisation and mechanical milking machines, progressed the dairy industry.

THE FIRST automatic telephone exchange in Australia (which didn't require an operator to connect calls) was opened in Geelong in 1912 and was followed by exchanges in Sydney and Melbourne in 1914.

Towns built on wealth & toil

Mineral wealth and natural resources saw some areas flourish while others failed. Many regional centres were once rich mining townships.

Above: Miners at Gympie circa 1873.

the FACTS!

CHARTERS TOWERS was so affluent in the 1890s that the local stock exchange opened 24 hours a day, seven days a week.

SILVER-LEAD DEPOSITS were found at Mt Isa, Queensland, by John Campbell in 1923.

THE LARGEST GOLD DEPOSITS in Queensland were at Mount Morgan, then called Ironstone Mountain. They made shareholders of the Mount Morgan Gold Mining Company very wealthy in the 1880s.

RICH BUT SHALLOW VEINS of gold were given the colloquial nickname of "jeweller's shops".

A WILD CYCLONE destroyed nearly every building in Townsville in 1867.

THE QUEENSLAND TOWN of Maryborough was home to two large timber mills and Walker's Ltd foundry, established to supply equipment to the Gympie goldfields.

TOWNSVILLE (QLD)

When the *Peruvian* was shipwrecked in the Coral Sea in 1846, its inhabitants drifted in a raft for 44 days until survivors washed up at Cleveland Bay, near today's Townsville. Only one, James Morrill, survived and lived with the Aborigines for seventeen years until, in 1863, settlers following Ludwig Leichhardt's route came upon a white man who said, in imperfect English, "Do not shoot me. I am a British object, a shipwrecked sailor". Grazing was established in the area around Ross Creek at a settlement first called Castletown, then renamed Townsville after Captain Robert Towns. Morill was offered land in the new settlement for just £4 as compensation for his struggles. The port became a landing point for thousands of miners heading to Charters Towers during the gold rush and Townsville flourished as the "Capital of the North".

CAIRNS (QLD)

James Cook named Trinity Bay in 1770, but it was not until 1876 that European settlement around Cairns began when it became the port for the Hodgkinson's goldfield. Timber-getting was an early industry until the discovery that sugar cane thrived in north Queensland's tropical regions led to a flourishing sugar industry. The population increased dramatically after a railway to the Herberton tin fields was established in 1884. Tea-growing and dairy farming are now also major industries.

ROCKHAMPTON (QLD)

In 1853, Charles and William Archer discovered and named the Fitzroy River and named the Beserker mountain range after a Norse hero. Two years later, they drove their sheep to the area and named it Gracemere. In 1856, William Wiseman found a site for a town and named it Rockhampton, after his birthplace in England. A small gold find at nearby Canoona brought prospectors from 1858 but proved unsustainable, and pastoral and mining industries became the backbone of Rockhampton, which is now known as Australia's beef capital.

NEWCASTLE (NSW)

Newcastle became the second British base on the mainland coast after coal was discovered in the region in 1791. Following the Castle Hill Uprising, Irish convicts were sent as part of a permanent settlement and put to work mining coal. By 1897, large-scale mining operations were underway and much of the prosperity of the Hunter Valley region can be attributed to coal mined from Newcastle, Maitland, Cessnock and Kurri Kurri. After a steelworks was constructed in Newcastle in 1915, limestone and iron from other parts of the continent were processed at Newcastle.

CHARTERS TOWERS (QLD)

Charters Towers (right) was once one of the most elegant gold-mining towns. Hugh Mosman and his Aboriginal servant Jupiter, along with George Clark and James Fraser, were the first to pan for gold near the Burdekin River, where Jupiter found alluvial gold. The diggings at Millchester soon became the city of Charters Towers, named for the mining warden of nearby Ravenswood, WS Charters, who logged the men's claim, and for the "towers" (tors — conical hills) near the city. In the boom years of the 1890s, citizens boasted Charters Towers was "The World" — because anything could be found there.

A fighting name

Bendigo was named after a local brawler nicknamed "Abednego" (shortened to Bendigo) after an English boxer. The name wasn't popular with everyone and at first the tent city was called Sandhurst.

Above, left to right: **Trade on the Murray River at Echuca relied on paddlewheelers and steamers; Elegant edifices in the gold town of Bendigo.**

GOULBURN (NSW)

The Goulburn Plains were first discovered by ex-convict Surveyor James Meehan in 1818, but the site was changed and the city gazetted in 1833. After convicts escaped from the Towrang penal settlement and terrorised settlers, travelling magistrates and soldiers were sent to dispense justice in Goulburn. Later, the town became the southern terminus for steam trains, and saddlery and blacksmithing propped up the thriving carriage trade. Some of the country's finest wool is grown around Goulburn.

BATHURST (NSW)

The first inland settlement of Australia was founded by George Evans in May 1815 and named after Earl Bathurst. It was first settled as grazing land, but when Edward Hargraves discovered gold at Ophir, 35 km away, "a complete mental madness … seized every member of the community", wrote the *Sydney Morning Herald*. Bathurst became the last major town before the goldfields. Its population doubled and many gracious public buildings and stores were erected. Once the gold diminished, Bathurst became a rich pastoral centre.

ECHUCA (VIC)

Located at the closest point to Melbourne on the Murray River, Echuca was destined to become a major inland port once paddlesteamers began to ply the river in the 1870s. Ex-convict Henry Hopwood realised its potential when he started a ferry service carrying sheep and cattle across the river, and later built the Bridge Hotel. The town became known as "the great shop" of the inland, and drovers and merchants flocked there. The name comes from an Aboriginal word meaning "meeting of the waters". In 1864, a railway meeting the port became a lifeline, carrying goods from paddlesteamer to the inland.

YASS (NSW)

Yass was established following discoveries by Hamilton Hume. According to legend, it received its name when Hume told an Aboriginal boy to climb a tree to look around and asked, "Can you see anything?" The boy replied, "Yass, plains". However, the name is more likely derived from the Aboriginal word for running water *yharr*. Hume was granted land on the Yass River as reward for his discovery of a new route over the Blue Mountains. The town is now "the fine wool hub of the world".

BEECHWORTH (VIC)

Beechworth was sighted by explorers Hume and Hovell in 1842 and later settled in the 1850s when land near the Ovens River was found to contain gold. The town was proclaimed in July 1853 and at its peak more than 50,000 people crammed into the district. Murray River trade and Beechworth's location between Melbourne and Sydney via Albury made it an important administrative centre.

BALLARAT (VIC)

Ballarat (below) had humble beginnings as a sheep run before Thomas Hiscock found gold at Buninyong in 1851, after which fortune hunters arrived in droves. Gold wealth adorned the town with civic beauty. After the gold rush, many people left the town and the city's leaders raced to establish secondary industries. The last gold mine in Ballarat closed in 1918.

the FACTS!

WITHIN A YEAR OF GOLD being found in Bendigo, more than 15,000 eager diggers had arrived. In the early days, just one bucketful of dirt could yield 23 kg of gold. By 1854, it was the largest goldfield in Victoria.

SUCCESSFUL Beechworth miner "Big" Johnson paid for golden shoes for the horse of his favourite politician during an electoral campaign. Each Easter the town's Golden Horseshoes Festival commemorates his generosity.

GOLD ALSO brought wealth to Castlemaine, Victoria, and by February 1852 more than 25,000 prospectors flocked to the Victorian township. A decade later, the town was flourishing.

Above: The historic Exchange Hotel in Kalgoorlie was built in 1900.

Ochre to copper

In 1869, a Cornish woman suggested that blue-green stains at an Aboriginal ochre pit near Cobar, NSW, were probably due to copper. She was correct and Cobar became an important mining town.

the FACTS!

TREATED WATER WAS sold to miners at the exorbitant price of two shillings a gallon — dearer than champagne at the time!

TRAGICALLY, while facing fierce criticism, O'Connor, the engineer behind the successful Kalgoorlie pipeline, committed suicide a month before the water began to flow.

GEELONG (VIC)

At first a squatter's settlement, Geelong grew rapidly on the wealth of the agricultural industry during the 1840s, when exports of mutton, wool and tallow were shipped around Australia and the world. It became a major centre for wool selling and exporting, soon surpassing Melbourne in exports and encouraging the *Geelong Advertiser* to boast:

> *Let Melbourne be the seat of Government, Geelong must be the pivot on which the commercial world turns. Melbourne may have an aristocracy, we shall have our Merchant Princes.*

It also became a busy landing port for fortune hunters heading to Ballarat in 1851, and became the third-largest city in Australia between 1851 and 1860.

COOLGARDIE (WA)

In the 1890s, Coolgardie, known as the "old camp" was the third-largest of Western Australia's towns. Today, the town has a more modest population. Arthur Bayley and William Ford discovered gold near the site of the city in 1892 and ushered in a decade of boom and bust mining. The town was formidably situated in the red-dirt district of gnarled scrub and extreme heat, and miners had to trek 180 km along a waterless track from Southern Cross. Many did not survive the journey. Typhoid ravaged the settlement and the lack of water made living standards unsanitary. A railway in 1896 and a permanent water pipeline from Perth in 1902 made conditions more bearable, but the population still plummeted in the early 20th century and by 1930 reached a low of just 100 residents. Deep-shaft mining for gold and nickel is once again placing Coolgardie at the centre of Western Australia's mining resources boom.

KALGOORLIE (WA)

Dan O'Shea, Paddy Hannan and Tom Flanagan discovered gold 40 km to Coolgardie's north-east in June 1893, bringing an influx of prospectors to the region. However, it was Wiliam Brookman and Sam Pearce who stumbled upon the real wealth in the area — the legendary Golden Mile, said to be the most lucrative square mile in the world. Water for the goldfields was obtained from bores and purified, but typhoid still killed hundreds of miners. Eventually Charles Yelverton O'Connor, Australia's chief engineer, planned a 563-km pipeline from a Perth reservoir to Kalgoorlie. In the 1960s, nickel deposits renewed mining in the area and new mining techniques continue to capitalise on Kalgoorlie–Boulder, Western Australia's "gold capital".

ALBANY (WA)

Although overlooked as a site for Western Australia's capital, Albany (below) was established as a military outpost and in the 1850s became an important port and coaling station until it was replaced by Fremantle in 1900. The original settlement, under the command of Major Edmund Lockyer, was named Frederick's Town, after King George's brother, Frederick Duke of York and Albany. Today, Albany is a heritage town and a popular holiday resort of the State's scenic South-West. The last operational whaling station in Australia was at Frenchman Bay in King George Sound; it closed in 1978.

Above: The National Wool Museum at Geelong, Victoria.

Above: After 1870, machine drills allowed mining deep underground.

Above: Historic architecture in Kapunda, South Australia.

KAPUNDA (SA)

Graziers Frederick Dutton and Charles Bagot opened the first copper mine near Kapunda in the north Mount Lofty Ranges in 1844, later forming the Kapunda Mining Company. The town was highly multicultural, with Cornish miners, Welsh engineers and smelters, Irish labourers and a small community of German farmers. When copper prices fell in the 1860s, Kapunda relied on agriculture as a means to keep the community prosperous.

GAWLER (SA)

Discovery of copper at Kapunda and Burra flowed through to the administrative town of Gawler, which became a resting town for bullock drivers carting loads of ore to Adelaide. More than 100 bullock drays a day passed through Gawler when mining in the area was at its peak. Gawler was planned by Colonel William Light, who designed Adelaide, but much to Light's chagrin was named after Governor George Gawler rather than its civic designer. James Martin was an influential founding father who established businesses in Gawler from 1848. By the 1860s, Gawler became known as a "colonial Athens". A famous resident was daring overland explorer John McKinlay.

QUEENSTOWN (TAS)

Queenstown (below) is another town founded on mining wealth, with the Mt Lyell mining enterprise extracting gold, silver and copper from the region.

THE BOOMING BURRA (SA)

When shepherds William Streair and Thomas Pickett made separate discoveries of a vein of copper running through the hills to Adelaide's north in 1845, the find drew miners from as far away as Cornwall, Wales and Germany. Two huge syndicates "the Nobs" (The Princess Royal Mining Association) and "the Snobs" (the South Australian Mining Association) pounced, but neither could afford the £20,000 required to buy the land. They pooled their resources then divided the land in half. The Burra Burra mine, also called the "Monster Mine" yielded almost £5 million worth of copper and made the shareholders of the South Australian Mining Association extremely wealthy. Although miners were paid less than 30 shillings a week, some shareholders accumulated almost £800,000 in dividends. There was no local smelting works so ore was taken to Port Adelaide on bullock drays and then shipped on wool ships (as ballast) to Swansea in Wales. When the ore ran out and the mine closed on 19 September 1877, Burra became a regional market town for the surrounding farmlands. Today, abandoned miners' cottages dot the arid landscape.

GOVE (NT)

Bauxite deposits estimated at 250 million tonnes were discovered in Gove in the 1950s. By 1968, the North Australian Bauxite and Alumina Company (Nabalco) had been established and was granted mining rights under the conditions that the company spend $100 million building the mine, township and port. Bauxite is used to make aluminium and other important bauxite cities are Weipa and Gladstone (Qld) and the Darling Range, Kwinana and Pinjarra (WA).

Gympie gold

Gold fever reached Gympie (below, shown in the 1870s) in 1867 and the town became Queensland's financial salvation. The Scottish Gympie mine was the largest and deepest, with underground roads more than 50 km long. By 1909, Gympie had 51 mining companies.

Below: Abandoned miners' cottages are a historical feature of the Burra region.

Immigration & deportation

Above: Today's Australia embraces and encourages multiculturalism.

Many settlers made their way to Australia from all around the globe, but Australia's immigration policy did not always provide a "fair go" for all emigrants. Race-based prejudice led to strict laws on who could enter the country; this later became known as the "White Australia Policy".

BYE BYE BLACKBIRD

From the 1860s, labourers from the Pacific Islands were brought to Australia to work in sugar cane plantations. They were known as "Kanakas" and many were threatened and coerced into coming or kidnapped, which at the time was euphemistically called "blackbirding". Pacific Islanders worked very hard for very low wages and by 1901 more than 57,000 lived in Australia. However, strict new laws aimed at reducing the number of non-whites meant that three-quarters of Australia's Melanesian workers were deported by 1906. Only those who had arrived before 1 September 1879 or those granted certificates of exemption under the *Immigration Restriction Act* were permitted to remain. Some of those deported had lived in Australia for more than twenty years.

Right: Pacific Islanders played a crucial role in the success of Queensland's cane industry, but received little appreciation.

INFAMOUS ACTS

An uprising at Lambing Flat goldfields in June 1861 led to more than 200 Chinese miners being injured when an angry European mob attacked them, cutting off their "pigtails", burning their tents and chasing them from the goldfields. Rather than the government attempting to address the miners' racism, riots were used as an example of why Asian immigration should be limited, and tough new laws were proposed. In 1901, the *Immigration Restriction Act* became the first act of Federal parliament. Immigrants were given a diction test in any language; those that failed were not permitted entry. This led to some Chinese immigrants taking tests in Gaelic, and, of course, failing. Later the same year, the *Pacific Islands Labourers Act* was passed. Both contributed to what would later become infamous as the "White Australia Policy".

Right: The Yi Yuan (Garden of Joy) Gardens in Bendigo, NSW, pay homage to the Chinese history of the region.

the FACTS!

ALL AUSTRALIAN-BORN PEOPLE, apart from Aborigines, were considered British subjects. Non-British subjects who were residents of the colonies could apply for naturalisation. An American named Timothy Gordon became the first person to be naturalised as a British subject in New South Wales in 1824. Foreigners who wanted to be naturalised had to swear an oath denying the authority of the Roman Catholic Church.

THERE WERE FOUR TIMES as many men as women in the cities in 1838, and twenty men for every woman in rural areas. At the time, marriage was encouraged as a way to keep women from turning to prostitution and men away from the rum. The British Government established a bounty system to help young, unmarried British women migrate to New South Wales.

BY 1841, when the practice of assigning convict labourers to settlers ceased, squatters and settlers needed cheap labour and immigration was encouraged.

IN 1855, a tax was imposed on all Chinese immigrants in an attempt to discourage them from coming to Victoria — as a result many Chinese disembarked in South Australia and walked to the Victorian diggings. By 1888, all colonies except Western Australia had entry charges to limit Chinese immigration.

BETWEEN 1911–1914 approximately 1785 youth migrants arrived from Britain. They were all aged 15–18 and were known as the "Dreadnought Boys".

Social reformers

Songs of the past

Tasmanian Aborigine Fanny Cochrane Smith tried to preserve Tasmanian Aboriginal language and songs with recordings made in 1899 and 1903.

In 1841, the price of wool dropped dramatically and many businesses and individuals became bankrupt. Many of those who had come seeking a better life were living on the streets and begging for food.

OLD AGE PENSIONS, workplace compensation for injuries and maternity leave were not available until the 1900s, so it was left to charitable individuals to help the less fortunate.

Left: **Caroline Chisholm was a highly respected social reformer.**

STARVING IN THE STREETS

To counter the shortage of women, by 1835 young single women were allowed free passage to Van Diemen's Land. Rampant unemployment and overcrowding in Britain encouraged young women to emigrate. Many were Irish or Scottish, fleeing famine in their homelands. Women had been promised a better life in Australia, but when they arrived there was no work and many were forced into prostitution. Henry Parkes, another social reformer, wrote, "*… hundreds of emigrants are at the present time starving in the streets of Sydney … By emigration regulations they are allowed to remain on board their respective vessels ten days after their arrival at Port Jackson … a young woman was turned out of one of these emigrant ships ... and was found by a policeman sitting on the Queen's wharf, and taken to the watchhouse. The next morning she was … charged with being drunk; and though she stated it was faintness … she was sentenced to sit one hour in the stocks*".

CAROLINE CHISHOLM

Caroline Chisholm arrived in Sydney in 1838 and was soon appalled by the conditions faced by some settlers, particularly young women, who received little government assistance and no welfare. She sought the help of Governor George Gipps to establish the Female Immigrant's Home shelter for women and wrote, "I devoted all my leisure in endeavouring to serve these poor girls, and felt determined, with God's blessing, never to rest until decent protection was afforded them". In 1849, she also set up the Family Colonisation Loan Society, which helped immigrants finance their journey to Australia. Settlers were able to take out a loan from the society, which they paid back once they arrived and began to earn a living. From 1839–1846 Mrs Chisholm arranged jobs for more than 11,000 new immigrants, including women, men and married couples. Caroline Chisholm died in 1877 after a lifetime of charity work.

the FACTS!

CHILDREN OFTEN became orphans when their parents were transported, so in 1846 Caroline Chisholm returned to England and helped reunite orphaned children who had been sent to workhouses with their families in Australia.

CHINESE IMMIGRANT and merchant Lowe Kong Meng became a prominent businessman and a founding member of the Commercial Bank of Australia. He arrived in Melbourne in 1853 and went on to help many less fortunate Chinese immigrants through his work with the See Yap and Gee Hing societies.

FROM 1915 (when the New South Wales Aboriginal Protection Board was given the power to remove children "for their own good") to 1938, more than 1400 children were taken from their parents.

EARLY SCOTTISH SETTLER Georgiana McRae treated the Bunorong people of Port Phillip Bay when they were ill and compiled a dictionary of Aboriginal words.

DAISY BATES (below), who fought against Aboriginal assimilation and dedicated 35 years of her life to Aboriginal welfare, was once married to the famous poet Breaker Morant, but left him after he was caught stealing.

DAISY BATES

Aboriginal people had few rights and were sent to reserves from the late 1800s to 1909. In August 1899, Daisy Bates (right) offered to investigate their circumstances and make a full report to *The Times.* From 1904 to 1919 she made many anthropological trips to live with Aborigines in South Australia and Western Australia and study and record their culture. Some Indigenous people came to know her as *Kabbarli* (grandmother) while *Woman's World* referred to her as "The Great White Queen of the Never Never". In 1934 she received the Order of the British Empire for her welfare work with Aborigines.

Above: Bushranger and folk hero, Ben Hall.

We'll fight but not surrender

Of course, not all people living in the colony wanted to be reformed. Some were content to roam the bush and steal whatever they could not obtain by honest means.

LEGENDS PORTRAY Australia's bushrangers as dashing folk heroes who were unfairly persecuted by the police. Some may have been, but others were simply escaped convicts or petty thieves who turned to robbing innocent settlers and stealing the proceeds of their hard labour.

THE WILD COLONIAL BOY

Dublin born John Donohoe (also known as Jack Donohue) was sentenced to transportation for life on 3 April 1823 for "intent to commit a felony". He arrived in Sydney Cove in January 1825. Almost three years later, he started his life as a bushranger. With two accomplices, he robbed bullock drays on the road between Sydney and Windsor. The men were caught, tried and sentenced to death — strangely twice on the same day (although once would have been enough!). His accomplices were hanged, but Donohue escaped from custody and became a notorious bushranger.

He led a gang that ranged country from Bathurst to Illawarra and the Hunter Valley. Donohue was eventually killed in gunfire between police and his gang in the Bringelly scrub near Campbelltown, during which he is reported to have taunted the police to "come on, using the most insulting and indecent epithets". His name lives on in various folk songs as Bold Jack Donohoe (pronounced Donahoo), the "Wild Colonial Boy".

BOLD BEN HALL

Ben Hall worked as a stockman before he took to bushranging after being wrongly arrested for armed robbery in 1862. Although acquitted, he was also under suspicion for the hold up of a gold escort in Eugowra. He was again released, but, on returning to his property, found his stock dead and his homestead torched; bitter, he turned to bushranging.

Hall's courtesy, courage, humour and hatred for informers made him a popular folk hero. His men were mounted on stolen racehorses and were able to out-gun and out-run the authorities. Friends and admirers also often alerted the gang to planned police raids. In 1863, Hall and his gang robbed Bathurst and Canowindra before turning their attentions to the Sydney–Melbourne Road and the Gundagi–Yass mail run. The *Felons Apprehension Act*, passed in April 1865, made it illegal for anyone to help or hide bushrangers, forcing them to keep moving from place to place.

The police issued a £1000 reward for Ben Hall's head and he was betrayed and killed on 5 May 1865 near Goobang Creek. Reports of his funeral mention that it was "rather numerously attended".

the FACTS!

BLACK DOUGLAS, an escaped mulatto Indian, was one of the most feared bushrangers of the goldfields near Maryborough in Victoria.

TEGG, an Aboriginal man, successfully tracked down the Aboriginal bushranger Musquito, but was disappointed that he didn't receive his promised reward, so he become a bushranger himself!

ONE TRADESMAN in Sydney created a line of clay pipes that were made to resemble John Donohoe's head, complete with a bullethole!

THE *FELONS APPREHENSION ACT 1865 (NSW)* meant bushrangers could be shot on sight.

AT LEAST TWO Chinese bushrangers were recorded. In 1859, one bailed up Mr Ball, of Cathcart in New South Wales, but was later scared off. Later, laundry man turned bushranger Sam Poo accosted people around Mudgee. He was hanged after he killed a police officer sent to capture him.

Left: A statue of Captain Thunderbolt graces the town of Uralla, where his body is buried.

CAPTAIN THUNDERBOLT

Frederick Ward roamed the New England area from 1865 under the name of Captain Thunderbolt, aided by a number of youths (the youngest, William Monkton, was just thirteen). Thunderbolt was an excellent horseman, did not use violence and was said to be gentlemanly in manner. He was careful not to rob armed coaches or towns that had police stations, instead bailing up mail coaches quite successfully until he was shot and killed in 1870.

Above, left to right: A wanted poster for the outlaws; The Kellys' armour was made out of the iron mould-boards of a plough.

DON'T RUIN CHRISTMAS

Renowned for being a gallant charmer, bushranger Frank McCallum preferred the more dashing name of Captain Melville. In 1851, he arrived in Port Phillip intending to seek his fortune on the gold diggings, but soon realised there was an easier way to strike it rich. When he bailed up two men on the Geelong road, taking £30, he later returned £10 because he didn't want to spoil the men's Christmas! Regardless, he and his friend William Roberts continued to rob passengers on the road right up until Christmas. Roberts was to be Melville's undoing; he boasted to a prostitute that he was a bushranger and the girl summoned the police. McCallum was captured and convicted to life on the hulk *Success* — his floating prison for 32 years. He eventually committed suicide by choking himself with a handkerchief in 1857. Legend has it his spoils are hidden somewhere in caves near Inglewood, Victoria.

ARMOURED GANGSTERS

The charismatic Kelly Gang were the last bushrangers — daring "sons of old Ireland" defending their family against all odds. When Mrs Kelly was sentenced to three years gaol for shooting Constable Fitzpatrick — who reported that Ned and Dan had shot him twice, although Ned was 400 km away — Ned, Dan and friends Steve Hart and Joe Byrne, were incensed.

Ned issued an ultimatum: release his mother or he would "be compelled" to use "colonial stratagems". It was to no avail, so Ned and his gang bailed up a police camp, killing three officers, after which the *Felons Apprehension Act* was reinstituted, meaning the men could be shot on sight. The gang robbed Faithful Creek Station, then Benalla and Jerilderie banks, before making plans to attack a special train carrying police to Beechworth to launch a raid on the gang.

The Kelly Gang's famous "last stand" occurred on 28 June 1880 in the small town of Glenrowan, Victoria, where the plan was to attack the train, steal the guns, shoot the officers and break into the gaol, freeing the prisoners and robbing banks and stores, then vanishing. The heavily armoured gang made the fatal mistake of freeing schoolteacher, Mr Curnow, who lit a flare on the railway tracks, alerting the police to the gang's intentions. Police made for Glenrowan Hotel, where they fired on the building. Ned was shot in the arm and retreated to the bush, where he fainted from blood loss. At dawn the next day (29 June) a man in thick armour appeared like an apparition in the fog and "staggered and reeled like a drunken man". Despite his heavy armour, he was shot in the legs and when "the mask was torn off" was revealed to be Ned Kelly himself. By 3 pm that day, when police set fire to the hotel — Steve, Dan and Joe, all suffering fatal, possibly self-inflicted bullet wounds, already lay dead inside. Ned Kelly (below) was taken to Melbourne Gaol Hospital until his trial on 28 October 1880. He was hanged on 11 November 1880.

the FACTS!

WHEN WILLIAM CRAIG found Captain Melville robbing a station, Melville, finding Craig had no money to steal, offered to share his spoils, saying, "*Well, old man. I'm Melville the outlaw — you've doubtless heard of me. I'm not flush of loose cash just now but I'll share what I have with you*".

SLIGHTLY BUILT Steve Hart was reported, by Chief Commissioner Standish, to be "in the habit of dressing himself in women's clothes and going through the country in this disguise..." This led to Ned's sister Kate being accused of crimes.

JOE BYRNE was addicted to opium, which was brought to the goldfields by Chinese traders.

BEFORE Ned Kelly was hanged on 11 November 1880, his mother visited him in gaol, telling him, "Mind you die like a Kelly, Ned!" As he walked to the gallows, he uttered his immortal, famous last words — "Ah well, I suppose it has come to this. Such is life!"

ON 14 OCTOBER 1854, John Bolton, Henry Garrett, Henry Marriott and Thomas Quinn, all ex-convicts from Port Arthur, held up the Bank of Victoria at Ballarat — without ammunition in their pistols. Unfortunately for the robbers, the lady of the Geelong boarding house they holed up in discovered their spoils and robbed the men herself!

Above: *Overlanders,* an 1860 watercolour by ST Gill.

Overlanders — drovers & swaggies

Bushrangers were not the only people roaming the bush — selectors and squatters drove sheep and cattle to market or to greener pastures, and swagmen "waltzed their matilda" in search of seasonal work such as shearing and mustering.

MANY SELECTORS FAILED to make a living on their plots and were forced to travel to find work to support their families. Employment was often irregular or seasonal, so men moved from place to place seeking work and carrying their belongings in a swag. Swags were made of water-resistant calico and, when unrolled, could be used as a groundsheet or a tent if slung between two trees. A "nose bag" contained the swaggie's rations and tobacco and he always carried a "billy can" of water to make tea.

The jobs swaggies might take on were varied. They might shear sheep; plough fields; clear timber and land; build fences, cattle yards or houses; or muster, brand and drove cattle. Some swagmen even offered to chop wood and do chores around the station in exchange for food and perhaps a little money. Squatters and graziers regularly moved their stock between their properties or drove them to market along stock routes that became known as "long paddocks". Droving work was popular with stockmen, boundary riders and swaggies. The Birdsville Track was used to drove stock from the Channel Country of Queensland to Marree in South Australia, and the Murranji Track to take cattle from Victoria River to Newcastle Waters in the Northern Territory and then on to Camooweal in Queensland. Stock routes are still used to help outback graziers provide enough feed for their stock.

TRICK OR TREAT?

With so many people wandering around the countryside, it became a tradition to be hospitable to travellers. Even very poor settlers gave food or a place to sleep to a swaggie, either through fear or generosity. Squatters, settlers and selectors usually gave swaggies enough meat, flour and tea to take them to the next property, even if they had no work available themselves. Anyone that did not help out a swaggie might later find their fences cut, a lamb missing, or parts of their run set alight.

SHEARERS' STRIKE

Shearers and other seasonal workers, such as wheat and cane harvesters, knew that they were a necessary part of Australian industries and expected fair pay for a long day's work. In 1891, when shearers felt that conditions and pay were not adequate, they formed a union and went on strike. After violence between shearers, police and soldiers, they held a meeting of the Australian Worker's Union in Barcaldine. This paved the way for the formation of the Australian Labor Party.

Left and right: **Swaggies carried few belongings and slept wherever they found shelter.**

the FACTS!

SHEARING IS ALL OVER *and we've all got our cheques/So it's roll up your swags boys, we're off on the track/The first pub we come to, we'll all have a spree/And everyone who comes along, it's "come and drink with me."* [Taken from *Click Go the Shears*]

SOME OF THE FIRST overlanders were Joseph Hawdon, John Gardiner and John Hepburn, who drove cattle south to Port Phillip from the Murrumbidgee River.

THE JARDINE BROTHERS, the Forrests and the Duracks were all well-known, competent drovers.

THE TERM "SWAG" was originally used by convicts and bushrangers to describe the booty of a robbery.

SOME SWAGGIES walked as far as 60 km in a day, seeking work.

WHEN THEY WERE not working, many shearers, swaggies and overlanders were drinking! Shanty hotels and sly grog shops sprang up and some workers spent all their hard-earned pay on grog. Alcohol was often diluted or mixed with something else. Sulphuric acid was used as a mixer by one publican!

Life in the big smoke

Above: Sydney crowds farewell soldiers leaving for the Boer War in 1899.

Although members of high society lived in the cities and followed sophisticated fashions and etiquette, in the early days of settlement Australia's cities were far from pretty; at worst they were very dirty. However, by the turn of the 20th century, living standards in Australian cities were among the highest in the world.

SMOG FROM BURNING COAL and shipbuilding industries, as well as sewage and other wastes made cities dirty and smelly and Sydney and Melbourne were also very crowded. At the time there were no indoor toilets, so toilets were "long-drop" pits in the backyard or chamber pots that were often emptied in alleyways. Many people in the cities also kept goats and chickens for milk and eggs, adding to the waste in the streets. There were no council rubbish collections, so when it rained, sewage and litter flowed down the streets. Epidemics of disease also swept through the cities. However, as the colonists became wealthy from the trade in wheat, wool, beef or goods, railways were built to suburbs beyond the cities' stench and people rushed to live in the cleaner suburbs. In this way, Australia's cities became the sprawling suburban metropolises they are today.

Above: People gather in the city of Launceston to celebrate the end of transportation in this watercolour and pencil on paper artwork attributed to artist Susan Fereday.

WORK IN THE CITIES

Until the depression of the 1890s, it was relatively simple to find work in the cities. People worked in metal work in the shipyards and railways, plied their trade as potters, seamstresses or "outfitters", or worked in hospitality industries such as the hotel or restaurant trade.

BEGGARS & BUMS

There was no income tax, but there were also no benefits or social services, so the sick, infirm or unemployed often begged for money. Soon, Friendly Societies were established and operated like insurance companies, paying their members an allowance if they became sick or sacked.

the FACTS!

TOUGH, RESOURCEFUL country people could not understand the "townies" who lived in the cities. The scorn of the country folk was reciprocated by city dwellers who looked down their noses at the rough-around-the-edges farmers.

SOME PEOPLE called Melbourne "Smellbourne" because of the unsanitary conditions.

CHILDREN IN THE CITIES were at risk from diphtheria, whooping cough, measles and scarlet fever because inoculation had not yet been invented. Some unfortunate parents might have buried all of their children within a matter of weeks.

PERTH did not have a public water supply until the 1890s. Typhoid and smallpox outbreaks killed many people in 1893–1894.

CAMELS AND CAMELEERS were common sights in Fremantle in the 1890s, so much so that laws were passed "restricting and regulating the driving of camels through the streets of the municipality".

BY THE MID 1900s, most Australian cities were prosperous centres of industry. Trams (below), automobiles, sewing machines and gas stoves were making domestic life easier for thousands of Australians and by 1914 Australia's living standards were among the highest in the world.

Education in the colonies

the FACTS!

SIR JOHN FRANKLIN developed the first primary schools in Van Diemen's Land in 1836–1842.

THE EDUCATION ACT of 1873 made school compulsory for children between the ages of eight to twelve in Victoria.

SCHOOL CHILDREN were punished by caning or whipping for making mistakes or bad behaviour. Some students were made to sit in the corner wearing a "dunce's cap".

DURING COLD WINTER months, students were often sent to school with wood for the fire and sometimes had to bring their own drinking water.

IN 1901, travelling schools were introduced to Queensland. New South Wales received its first travelling school in 1908. Teachers travelled from place to place in a horse-drawn cart and conducted lessons on the verandahs of homesteads or in tents. New South Wales' first travelling teacher, Albert Biddle, spent a week at each of four remote cattle stations, setting lessons for the children to complete in the three weeks he was away.

In the early days of settlement, children were expected to help out on properties or to work and most did not go to school. In most States, school was only made compulsory in the late 1870s, when fees were reduced so that poor children could receive an education.

ONLY AREAS that had a high population of children had a government school. In smaller regions, churches or community members ran the school. Many areas had no school at all! When schools first began to be established, most were only open every second day or in the afternoons and many children attended school for just two years. Some of the wealthier squatter families paid a governess — a young, unmarried teacher who would live with the family — to teach their children, but many others were too poor for this, and, as they were on isolated properties where there was no school nearby, the children simply did not go to school.

COMPULSORY SCHOOLING

At first, all schools charged a fee, which many parents could not afford, but when education became compulsory the fees were reduced.

Not everyone was happy about compulsory schooling. Many selectors feared that their children would be taught to despise farm life and move to the city; others wondered how they would cope without the extra hands around the farm. However, most of them wanted their children to have a good education and the chance to learn to read, write and improve themselves.

Mostly, all of the children, no matter their age, were taught in one large class but were set separate lessons. Classes were different for boys and girls, with girls learning sewing and other useful domestic tasks while boys learned skills such as technical drawing or graphics. Children wrote their lessons and did sums on slates (top left) — thick pieces of polished stone that acted like small blackboards and had to be wiped clean after each lesson. Older students progressed to using an ink pen and writing in books.

Left, top to bottom: **Classrooms were sparsely equipped with a blackboard, maps and books, and children often had to share desks and educational material; A typical teacher's desk reconstructed at Rockhampton Historical Museum; Children were usually taught in one large class.**

Fashion & language

Settlers imported fashionable styles and etiquette from England and Europe, but most were impractical for the Australian climate — especially for country people. Poorer settlers could not afford to spend money on finery or entertaining, which increased the social divide between the civilised wealthy squatters and the settlers and selectors.

COUNTRY WOMEN sweltered in ankle-skimming skirts made of heavy serge with long petticoats or bloomers underneath. Often the swirling skirts were a fire hazard because most settlers cooked over open fires. Long-sleeved blouses with high collars were tucked into the skirt and aprons were worn to keep the clothes clean. In cold weather, a shawl or cloak covered the shoulders. Settlers usually had large families of around thirteen children, so clothes were "hand-me-downs". Clothes that were out of fashion or needed repairing were patched up, reworked or cut down and sewn into children's clothes. Many children went barefoot because few parents could afford to buy shoes. Most women sewed their own clothes and the average wardrobe consisted of three sets of "work clothes" and one set of "Sunday best", for attending church or special occasions. Ladies of the mid-1800s, who rarely had to do heavy work, were able to wear clothes of a lighter, less durable material that was held out from the body with hoops or a stiff frame called a crinoline. Sometimes 6–8 petticoats were worn to make the skirts full. Underneath the bodice was a corset, designed to cinch in the waist. Zips had not yet been invented, so servants had to button or lace up ladies' dresses. Well brought up women were also rarely seen in public without a sunhat or parasol.

"STERLING" GENTLEMEN, who had been born in England, usually wore the conservative frock coat, shirt and breeches of Europe. "Currency lads" born in the colony were more likely to abandon the three-piece suit combination in favour of moleskins, a shirt with rolled up sleeves, a bandana around the neck and a hat made out of woven together cabbage-tree palm fronds.

STRINE & SLANG

Some of the convicts brought "flash" cockney rhyming slang to the colony, which had to be translated to the officers and upper-class settlers, who did not understand it. Gradually, as Australian idiom grew, rhyming slang such as to "have a Captain Cook" (look) came into common use. Settlers came up with some novel ways to describe animals and objects in the new land. The Laughing Kookaburra became known as the "settler's clock" and rabbits were jokingly called "underground mutton". Sometimes phrases were used to disguise insults, for instance "pure merinos" was used as slang for exclusives who thought they had "purer" blood than freed convicts. Aboriginal words such as "walkabout" were adopted into common use. Today, Australian English is sometimes referred to as "Strine", which pokes fun of Australians' nasal drawl and tendency to shorten or slur words.

Above: Ladies enjoy high tea in a Gympie garden in 1907, wearing hats adorned in the feathery fashion.

the FACTS!

BOYS AND GIRLS both wore dresses until they were about three or four years old, when boys progressed to wearing shorts and jackets and girls to three-quarter-length dresses. Longer pants and dresses were only for older children.

UNDERNEATH their voluminous petticoats and crinoline women wore crotchless pantaloons, because they could not pull down their pantaloons to go to the toilet!

A NEWSPAPER REPORTED in 1864 that one little girl was blown into the air and carried quite a distance after a gust of wind caught under her crinoline!

ETIQUETTE DICTATED that even those living in the most decrepit huts (below) lay out a "proper" table for guests. Often a hostess's most prized and expensive possessions would be china and silverware, much of which would have been collected over the years or given to her for her "hope chest" — a box of linen and other household goods young women gathered in anticipation of marriage.

Finance, trade & commerce

Many settlers prospered, despite somewhat erratic banking and monetary systems hashed together with various types of currency, including rum and promissory notes.

A CURRENCY OF OUR OWN

In the early days of settlement, Australia had no currency of its own. For a while, the most common currency in the colony was rum! However, most financial matters were handled by promissory notes, which were handwritten credit notes from government officials or a mix of English currency and coins from other countries. Spanish dollars or "holey dollars" (right), so called because they had the centre (the "dump") cut out, were also used from 1814. The British pound sterling was adopted throughout the British Empire in 1826 and English coins began to be minted in Australia. In 1855, when the Royal Mint was established in Sydney, it began to move towards creating an Australian currency. Following Federation in 1901, the Commonwealth Department of Treasury took over, but it was not until 1910 that the first truly Australian silver and copper coins were produced. From Federation to the 1920s, the Treasury issued Australian notes, which were printed by the Commonwealth Bank until 1960, when the Reserve Bank took over printing.

the FACTS!

THE BANK of New South Wales (renamed Westpac in 1982) was Australia's first bank. The bank was established by Governor Lachlan Macquarie in 1817.

SHIPPING AGENTS and import/export merchants arranged for wool sold at local markets to be exported overseas and banks were set up to finance shipping. Many men became dock workers (below) and Sydney, Melbourne, Hobart, Gladstone and Darwin became busy ports.

THE RECESSION OF 1891 saw many people who had over-borrowed money in Britain go bust. Banks started closing, businesses went bankrupt and many people became unemployed.

LABOUR REFORM, such as the establishment of the Commonwealth Court of Conciliation and Arbitration (a mediation body between employers and workers) and the introduction of a minimum wage in 1907, allowed industry to flourish.

MAKING & SAVING MONEY

In the 1700s and 1800s, cottage industries concentrated on producing goods required by the fledgling colony, such as bricks, beer and textiles. The influx of colonists after the gold rush saw demand increase, and from 1864 to 1894, some industries rapidly expanded. Sydney's western suburbs became known for small factories specialising in metal products, printing, tobacco products and food, drink and textile manufacturing.

The gold rush sparked a massive boom in the colony, which flourished until the 1890s (when the depression began). Gold wealth was channelled into impressive architecture and a rise in expensive imported wares. Banks and stock exchanges were also built, and by 1852 the University of Sydney had been funded.

From Federation to World War I, Australia enjoyed a period of strong economic growth, and exports doubled between 1901 and 1913. Private banks had been established since the early 1800s, but they loaned off their own capital and many of them hit the wall. In 1893, twelve banks closed their door in the space of just six weeks. To increase financial security, in 1911 the Federal Government formed the Commonwealth Bank (CBA) to issue notes of credit that could be backed by the resources of the nation. This solved the currency problem. Notes issued by the CBA, and later the Reserve Bank, were accepted as legal tender, although their exchange value varies internationally.

Below: **A recreated bank clerk's office at the Mareeba Heritage Museum.**

Sport, art & entertainment

Above: Popular author Miles Franklin.

Life in the city and the bush was very different, however both city folk and settlers needed some form of entertainment after the end of a long day's work. There was no television or radio, so books, literature and sport were an important part of recreation. Socialising was done at church or when "calling" on neighbours.

Above: Some ladies, such as Ellis Rowan, painted Australian flora as a pastime.

IN RURAL AREAS, male settlers and selectors amused themselves by drinking in sly rum shops, holding boxing and horse-racing tournaments, hunting and playing "folk" football, which was similar to today's Australian Rules but used a round ball and larger teams. Farmers would also compete in wood-chopping and ploughing competitions. Bush folk music had its origins in the defiant convict songs of old, and ballads such as *Waltzing Matilda* and *Click Go the Shears* surpassed earlier convict tunes in popularity.

IN THE CITIES, wealthier settlers indulged in rowing, sailing regattas, opera and card playing tournaments. Church was an important social occasion and men and women dressed in all their finery for their weekly worship. Playing piano, sketching and doing embroidery as well as playing cards or board games and reading were at-home entertainments for ladies.

LITERATURE & THEATRE

Many books focused on the lives of former convicts or were about life as a squatter or a remote selector, such as Ethel Turner's *Seven Little Australians* and Marcus Clarke's *For the Term of His Natural Life*. In 1880, the *Sydney Bulletin* was founded — it encouraged Australian writers to engage in the task of writing literature about Australia. The *Bulletin* frequently published Australian poets and authors such as Banjo Paterson, Henry Lawson and Adam Lindsay Gordon. Authors' works were also often serialised in the newspapers. In 1901, 22-year-old Stella Maria Sarah Franklin, writing under the male pen name of Miles Franklin, penned one of the most acclaimed Australian novels — *My Brilliant Career.* It told the story of a brave, headstrong girl growing up in the Australian outback, who longed for a career as a writer. At the time, women were largely expected to marry young and raise a family and working was frowned upon. The book was later made into a film and its author became the benefactor of Australia's most prestigious literary award.

AUSTRALIAN THEATRE owes much of its origins to the gold rush, when extravagant travelling "shows" kept miners entertained. During the gold rush, George Coppin opened theatres in Melbourne and in 1874 JC Williamson was bought to Australia. Williamson would later control almost all the large theatres in the country. By the 1830s in Sydney, visiting musicians were performing vocal and orchestral concerts and choral societies began to be established in the 1850s. Australia pioneered early filmmaking and in 1896 French filmmaker Maurice Sestier recorded short local events such as the Melbourne Cup. In 1906, the *Story of the Kelly Gang* became the first full-length feature film.

the FACTS!

SOME PEOPLE would travel more than 100 km to go to a local ball.

IN 1803, Australia's first cricket match was held.

A NEW FOOTBALL CODE, at first called Victorian Rules (but now known as Aussie Rules) was played from the late 1850s. The first interstate match was in 1908.

SIX BATHING POOLS were open in St Kilda, Melbourne, by 1868. The NSW ban on daytime swimming in the sea was lifted in 1906, when the Bondi Surf Bathers' Lifesaving Club was formed. The first person lifesavers rescued was Charles Kingsford Smith, who would later become a famous Australian aviator.

AUSTRALIA'S first large horse-racing event was held in 1810 in Hyde Park, and the first Melbourne Cup was run in 1861. The first winner, Malvolio, is pictured below.

Many States — one Commonwealth

Above: The Australian Coat of Arms.

After the 1870s, once the soon-to-be States were joined in communication and trade by telegraph and railway lines, it began to seem sensible for all Australians to share the same laws and government.

SIX SEPARATE British Colonies (New South Wales, South Australia, Western Australia, Queensland, Tasmania and Victoria) existed in Australia prior to the nation's Federation in 1901. Each had their own laws and government but all were controlled by the British Empire. When Britain withdrew its troops from Australia in 1870, leaving the six colonies responsible for the nation's defence, people began to wonder how six separate States could fend off an attack if one occurred. In 1883–1884, when Germany annexed north-eastern New Guinea, the mood in the Australian colonies became ever more wary. Prominent politicians began to call for Federation to join the States into one nation.

Federation had been discussed by various politicians from as early as 1842, but in the late 1880s men such as Henry Parkes and Alfred Deakin championed the cause with popular slogans such as "one people, one destiny". A detailed plan for a commonwealth was drawn up in 1890.

"YES" TO MERGING

In 1891, the first constitutional convention was held, with delegates from each State and from New Zealand in attendance. Further conventions were later held in Adelaide, Sydney and Melbourne. After drafting a constitution that gave some idea of how the States would be governed, the delegates agreed on a draft law to set up a commonwealth. Despite agreeing to the draft bill, politicians in all States were still unsure whether federating was the right thing to do. Smaller States worried they would be absorbed into the larger colonies and lose a lot of their power. Larger colonies were concerned they would be "propping up" the smaller States. Sydney was a tariff-free port and worried federating would mean taxes and tariffs were imposed on imports (as they were in some other colonies). In June 1898, referendums were held in South Australia, Tasmania, Victoria and New South Wales. Although all but New South Wales passed the referendum, not enough people had voted and the referendum failed. In 1899, premiers met again to discuss Federation; this time, Queensland also attended. Following this meeting, referendums were held in all States apart from Western Australia, and the majority voted yes to Federation.

Below: Members of the Australian Federation Convention in 1891.

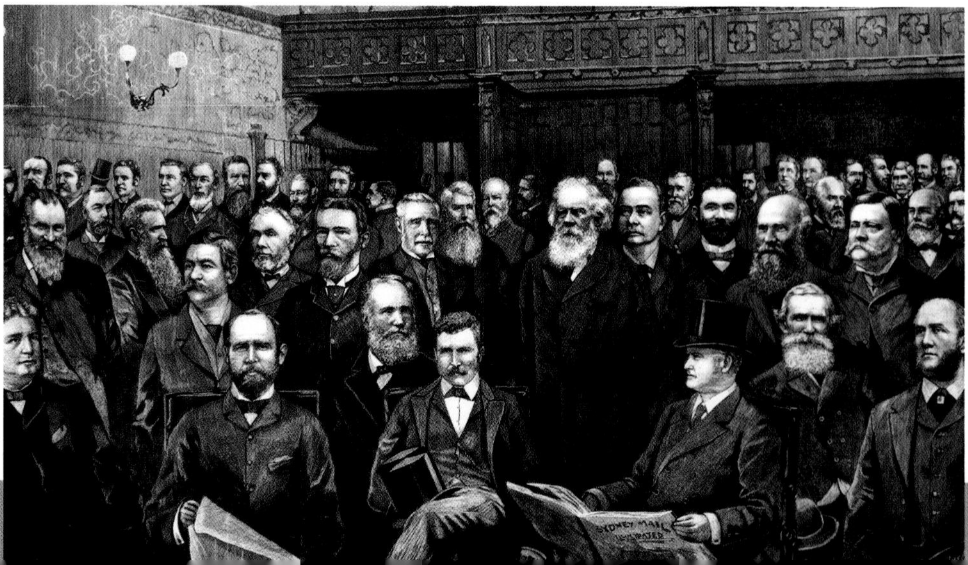

the FACTS!

THE FEDERAL COUNCIL OF AUSTRALIA was set up in 1885 but it had no independent funds or real power and New South Wales refused to join.

DELEGATES FROM New Zealand attended the first constitutional convention in 1891, but decided not to join the commonwealth.

FIVE FEDERATION CONVENTIONS were held in 1890, 1891, twice in 1897 and in 1898.

AUSTRALIA'S FIRST governor-general was the former governor of Victoria Lord Chamberlain, the Earl of Hopetoun.

ALFRED DEAKIN (below) speaking at the Federation Conference in 1890, said *"in this country, we are separated only by imaginary lines ... we are a people one in blood, race, religion and aspiration".*

Above, left to right: Federation celebrations held in the streets of Queensland in 1901; Parliament first sat in Melbourne's Royal Exhibition Building; Edmund Barton, Australia's first prime minister.

ONE FEDERATED NATION

The British Parliament agreed to the formation of the Australian nation in July 1900. At the same time, Western Australians voted in a referendum and also said yes to Federation. Consequently, on 1 January 1901, the Australian Commonwealth was forged out of the Federation of the six States. Less than six months later, on 9 May 1901, the first Commonwealth Parliament was opened by the Duke of Cornwall and York in Melbourne's Royal Exhibition Building. Commonwealth Parliament would sit in Melbourne for a further 26 years, until the Australian Capital Territory was established and Canberra became the new seat of Australian Federal Parliament.

Above: Tom Roberts' *The Big Picture* shows the Commonwealth Parliament being opened by HRH the Duke of Cornwall and York (later King George V) in 1901. It hangs in Parliament House Canberra.

Below: Canberra, in the Australian Capital Territory, was set aside as the seat of Federal Parliament in 1911. Old Parliament House (pictured) was built in 1927 and Parliament House in 1988.

the FACTS!

ALFRED DEAKIN, a Victorian lawyer, advocated Federation. He argued that delegates for the convention should be elected and during the 1890s he and Edmund Barton (of New South Wales) were tireless campaigners for Federation. So passionate were these two men that Edmund Barton became Australia's first prime minister and Alfred Deakin, the second.

SIR SAMUEL GRIFFITH is said to have drafted Australia's first constitution as he cruised down the Hawkesbury River on board the *Lucinda* in 1891; however, some people argue that he actually rewrote a draft written by Andrew Inglis Clarke, and made quite a hash of it! It ended up a functional but rather uninspiring document.

THE CONSTITUTION stipulates that the Commonwealth Parliament is "bicameral", that is, it is made up of two houses — one that represents the people of the nation, and one representing the people voting by State. The consent of both houses is required for any law to pass.

THE OPENINGS of the first Commonwealth Parliament in Melbourne 1901, Old Parliament House in Canberra 1927, and the current Parliament House in 1988, have all occurred on 9 May.

Above: Soldiers are honoured Australia-wide.

The Great War — your country needs you!

Australia was beginning to forge a national identity in the early 1900s, but despite being so far away from Europe, sentiment and history still bound the newly federated nation to the "Mother Country". For this reason, in 1914 when Britain declared war on Germany, Australia was quick to offer allegiance and enthusiastically volunteered troops.

AT THE TIME, Prime Minister Joseph Cook expressed a notion common to Australians, saying, "Australia is part of the Empire right to the full. When the Empire is at war, so is Australia at war". Australia's defence forces were ill-prepared for war, despite compulsory military service being initiated in 1910, but men still rushed to enlist. Most thought the war would be over quickly and some saw it as a chance to see the world. Australia's population was just five million at the time, but more than 416,000 men enlisted — by the war's end more than 60,000 had lost their lives and another 166,819 were injured.

THE FREEDOM TO CHOOSE

World War I also reinforced Australia's democracy. Terrible losses at the Somme meant more soldiers were required, which prompted Prime Minister William Hughes to hold a referendum on conscription in 1916. The referendum was defeated, as was another in December 1917, but Australian men, bound by a sense of duty, continued to volunteer. Australian troops remained the only all-volunteer army throughout the war and fought gallantly at Amiens, Poziéres, Tobruk and El Alamein. One British historian wrote they became "the spearhead of the British Army".

COURAGE IN CARNAGE

The battle of WWI that remains etched into the consciousness of every Australian, and is commemorated annually in Australia on 25 April (Anzac Day), is the hopeless misery of Gallipoli. Approximately 2300 Australians lost their lives in a single day on the steep slopes of the Gallipoli Peninsula. Altogether, 8709 Australians and 2701 brave New Zealanders of the combined Australian New Zealand Army Corps (ANZAC) perished in the campaign, which lasted from April to December until Allied troops were withdrawn. Other theatres of death were Passchendaele, Bullecourt, Polygon Wood, Ypres and Fromelles, in France and Belgium, where the green fields saw some of the most bloody, brave, but ultimately pointless, trench warfare ever experienced. Often, thousands were killed for the gain of just a few metres, which were quickly lost again. In just a half hour in July 1916, more than 5000 men of the Australian Fifth Division were slaughtered in the muddy trenches of Fromelles.

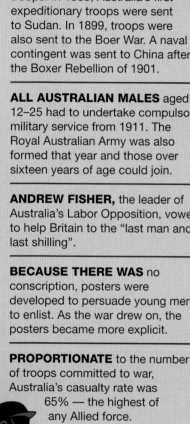

the FACTS!

WWI WAS NOT the first war to which Australians had committed troops. In 1885, Australia's first expeditionary troops were sent to Sudan. In 1899, troops were also sent to the Boer War. A naval contingent was sent to China after the Boxer Rebellion of 1901.

ALL AUSTRALIAN MALES aged 12–25 had to undertake compulsory military service from 1911. The Royal Australian Army was also formed that year and those over sixteen years of age could join.

ANDREW FISHER, the leader of Australia's Labor Opposition, vowed to help Britain to the "last man and last shilling".

BECAUSE THERE WAS no conscription, posters were developed to persuade young men to enlist. As the war drew on, the posters became more explicit.

PROPORTIONATE to the number of troops committed to war, Australia's casualty rate was 65% — the highest of any Allied force.

Left: Guilt tactics and fear were used in "call up" posters to help recruit more volunteers. There was no conscription for troops in World War I.

Coming of age
— a sense of nationhood

Above: A view from the trenches during WWI. Sometimes trenches were just metres apart.

Above: The Australian War Memorial commemorates the sacrifices soldiers made.

That Australians hold a national holiday for one of the Anzac's most unsuccessful campaigns seems strange to the rest of the world. But on the beaches of Turkey and the fields of Flanders, a national identity and reputation was forged. The world finally realised that the "colonies" had become one proud, progressive country.

AUSTRALIAN SOLDIERS came to be known as brave, fearless and determined fighters with a larrikin streak, a laconic adherence to discipline and a deep loyalty to their "cobbers" (mates). English war correspondent Philip Gibbs wrote:

> *I liked the look of them. Dusty up to their eyes in summer, muddy up to their ears in winter — scornful of discipline for discipline's sake, but desperate fighters ... and looking at life with frank, curious eyes and a kind of humorous contempt for death.*

AUSTRALIA'S OFFICIAL WAR HISTORIAN, Charles Bean summed up the Australian soldier's contribution to nationhood, writing:

> *When the AIF first sailed it left Australia a nation that did not yet know itself. Even the first Australian Division entered its first battle not knowing what manner of men Australians were. The people of the six States which formed the Commonwealth were much divided. Many an Australian had no confidence in his people for any big enterprise ... And then, during four years in which nearly the whole world was tested, the people of Australia looked on from afar at three hundred thousand of their own nation struggling amongst millions from the strongest and most progressive people of Europe and America. They saw their own men — those who had dwelt in the same street or been daily travellers in the same railway trains — flash across the world's consciousness like a shooting star ...*

21ST-CENTURY SETTLERS

Through the efforts of hard-working settlers and courageous troops, Australia received new standing in the world. Australians were no longer criminals or "nut browns" from the furthest outreaches of the Empire, but a proud, resourceful people from a nation built on toil, honesty and sacrifice. On a foundation created by ancient Aboriginal warriors, determined settlers, reformed convicts and larrikin soldiers, today's Australians — some of them 21st-century settlers migrating to this nation — build their promising future.

the **FACTS!**

ON 11 NOVEMBER 1918 emissaries for Germany's Kaiser Wilhem signed an armistice, signifying the end of WWI. Each year, on the eleventh hour of the eleventh day of the eleventh month (11 am on 11 November) people around the globe honour the millions of soldiers who fell, with a minute's silent reflection. Lest we forget.

FOLLOWING THE WAR, there were still many issues that the young nation had to attend to, such as giving Aborigines the right to vote and reversing some of the racist policies that were supported at Federation.

MANY OF THE VIRTUES espoused by Australia's settlers, such as humour in adversity, contempt for class systems and a sense of a "fair go" for all are evident in Australian culture and values today.

Web links & further reading

PUBLICATIONS

Angus & Robertson Concise Australian Encyclopedia, Revised Edition, Angus & Robertson, North Ryde, NSW, 1986

Basset, J. (Ed). *Great Southern Landings: An Anthology of Antipodean Travel*, Oxford University Press, Melbourne, Australia, 1995

Barwick, J. & J. *Australian History in the 20th Century*, Heinemann Library, Reed Educational & Professional Publishing, Port Melbourne, Victoria, 2000

Barwick, J. & J. *Exploration and Expansion*, Heinemann Library, Port Melbourne, Vic, 1999

Bradley, P. *The Making of Australia: Soldiers, Sailors and Mutiny*, Bay Books, Kensignton, NSW, 1983

Brasch, N. *The Early Ocean Explorers*, Reed International Books, Port Melbourne, Australia, 2005

Burke, E. & Mirams, S. *Australian History: Dreamtime to the Great War*, Oxford University Press, South Melbourne, 2001

Cannon, M. *The Exploration of Australia*, Reader's Digest, Sydney, Australia, 1987

Cannon, M. *The Roaring Days*, Today's Australia, Melbourne, 1998

Child, M. *Australia's Second Century 1901–present*, Murray David Publishing, Newtown, New South Wales, 2004

Clark, M. *A Short History of Australia*, Penguin Books, Sydney, Australia, 1992

Clark, M. Hoopers, M. & Ferrier, S. *History of Australia*, Scholastic, Gosford, NSW, 1995

Cox, K. *Amazing Facts About Australia's Early Explorers*, Steve Parish Publishing, 2008

De Vries, S. *Great Pioneer Women of the Outback*, HarperCollinsPublishers, Sydney, New South Wales, 2005

Fraser, B. (Ed) *The Macquarie Encyclopedia of Australian Events*, The Macquarie Library, Macquarie University, NSW, 1997

Gard, S. *Settling Australia: The Settlers*, Macmillan Education Australia, South Yarra, Vic, 1988

Gard, S. *Settling Australia: The Convicts*, Macmillan Education Australia, South Yarra, Vic, 1988

Guile, M. *Little Felons: Child Convicts 1788–1853*, Heinemann Library, Harcourt Education, Port Melbourne, Victoria, 2005

Hocking, G. *Robbery Under Arms: Dark Days on the Highways*, Waverton Press, Waverton, NSW, 2004

Hosty, K. *Convicts and Early Settlers 1788–1850*, Macmillan Education Australia, South Yarra, Vic, 2000

Jones, C. *A Time Machine Through Australia 1788–1901: Back to Adelaide*, Macmillan Library, South Yarra, Victoria, 2004

Jones, C. *A Time Machine Through Australia 1788–1901: Back to Port Phillip*, Macmillan Education Australia, South Yarra, Victoria, 2004

Jones, C. *A Time Machine Through Australia 1788–1901: Back to Sydney Cove*, Macmillan Education Australia, South Yarra, Victoria, 2004

Jones, C. *A Time Machine Through Australia 1788–1901; Back to Swan River*, Macmillan Education, South Yarra, Victoria, 2004

Jones, K. *Free Settlers 1891–1939*, Macmillan Education Australia, South Yarra, Vic, 2000

Parry, A. *The Gold Rushes: Riots, Robberies and Rebellions*, Macmillan Education Australia, South Yarra, Vic, 2007

Parry, A. *The Gold Rushes: Everyday Life on the Goldfields*, Macmillan Education Australia, South Yarra, Vic, 2007

Readers Digest, *Book of Historic Australian Towns*, Readers Digest (Australia) Pty Ltd, Surry Hills, NSW 2001

Sheppard, B. *Early Settlers: Life in a Harsh New Land*, Echidna Books, Port Melbourne, Vic, 2006

WEBSITES

www.gutenberg.net.au/explorers.html
www.australiassouthwest.com
www.rahs.org.au
www.librariesaustralia.nla.gov.au
www.cultureandrecreation.gov.au
www.adb.online.anu.edu.au/adbonline.htm

AUSTRALIAN MUSEUMS

National Museum of Australia
Lawson Crescent, Acton Peninsula, Canberra, ACT, 2600

Australian Museum
6 College Street, Sydney, NSW, 2010

Melbourne Museum
Nicholson St, Carlton, Melbourne, Vic, 3053

Queensland Museum
Grey St, South Brisbane, Qld, 4000

Museum of Sydney
Cnr Phillip and Bridge Streets, Sydney, NSW, 2000

Western Australian Museum
Perth Cultural Centre, James Street, Perth, WA, 6000

Museum & Art Gallery of the Northern Territory
Conacher St, Bullocky Pt, Darwin, NT, 0820

South Australian Museum
North Terrace, Adelaide, SA, 5000

State Library of Tasmania
91 Murray Street, Hobart, Tas, 7000

Glossary

ALLUVIAL GOLD Gold found in river beds or deposited by water.

ARABLE Land capable of producing crops by means of ploughing.

BALEEN Flat, flexible plates of keratin in the upper jaw of some whales.

BLACKSMITH A person who makes horseshoes and shoes horses.

BURGEONING Rapidly growing.

CARPENTER A person who erects and fixes houses and other structures.

COLONY A group of people who leave their native country to form a new land. A settlement subject to, or connected with, a parent state.

COMPULSORY Obligatory, forced.

CONTINENT A main land mass surrounded entirely by water.

CONVICT In Australian history, a person transported to the colonies from Britain to serve out a prison sentence.

COOPER Someone who makes or repairs casks, barrels, tubs, etc.

DIALECT A special variety or branch of a language.

ETIQUETTE Accepted requirements of social behaviour, as established within communities.

FELON Someone who has committed a crime.

FORMIDABLE Of alarming strength, size or difficulty.

HULKS Decaying old ships.

IDIOM A form of expression unique to a language, usually with a meaning other than its obvious one.

INCORRIGIBLE A person thought to be beyond reform; willful and uncontrollable.

INDIGENOUS Native to a particular country or location, i.e. Indigenous Australians.

INFAMOUS Having a bad reputation; known for being bad.

INHABITANT A person or animal that inhabits a place.

INOCULATION Vaccination.

MAORI Indigenous Polynesian people of New Zealand.

MASON Someone who builds or works with stone.

MORSE CODE A system of dots, dashes and spaces used in telegraphy and signalling to represent the letters of the alphabet or numerals.

NAVIGATOR Someone who conducts explorations by sea or is skilled in the navigation of ships or aircraft.

NOMAD A person without a fixed home, who moves from place to place according to the availability of food or shelter.

NOTORIETY Being widely known or well known.

POPULOUS Well populated.

PROMISSORY NOTES Handwritten credit notes from government officials, used in place of money.

PROSPEROUS Successful; of good fortune.

RECONCILIATION Settling a lingering dispute or grievance.

REFORM To change and move away from a dishonest way of life.

SLANG Informal speech using words or phrases unique to a particular country or area.

THE BENDS A sometimes fatal disorder caused by surfacing from deep water too rapidly; usually found in divers.

VITICULTURE Cultivation of grapevines.

WATTLE-AND-DAUB HUTS Early pioneers' dwellings built by shaping moist mud over a framework of wattle twigs and then leaving it to dry.

WHEELWRIGHT Someone who makes or repairs wheels and wheeled carriages.

IMPORTANT DATES

>60,000 YEARS AGO — Aboriginal people inhabit Australia.

1606 — Willem Janz is first European to land on the mainland.

1642–1643 — Abel Tasman discovers Tasmania and New Zealand.

1770 — James Cook claims eastern Australia for Britain.

1788 — Governor Arthur Phillip and the First Fleet arrive in Botany Bay.

1790 — The Second Fleet brings more convicts and the NSW Corps.

1791 — The Third Fleet brings more convicts, including Irish convicts.

1803–1804 — Settlement at Risdon Cove, Tasmania, established.

1808 — Governor Bligh is deposed in the Rum Rebellion.

1810 — Governor Lachlan Macquarie replaces the NSW Corps with the 73rd Regiment.

1813 — Blaxland, Lawson and Wentworth cross the Blue Mountains, opening up settlement.

1824 — Moreton Bay penal settlement established (Qld).

1825 — Van Diemen's Land (Tas) becomes a separate colony.

1829 — James Stirling establishes settlement near the Swan River, (WA).

1830 — Port Arthur prison established.

1835 — John Batman finds and settles the site for Melbourne.

1836 — Adelaide (SA) is proclaimed.

1842 — Moreton Bay (Qld) is opened for settlement.

1851 — Gold is discovered in NSW and Victoria.

1854 — The Eureka Stockade, Ballarat (Vic).

1863 — Pacific labourers brought to Australia.

1871 — Overland Telegraph links Australia to the world.

1901 — Federation creates a nation.

1909 — Canberra is set aside as the nation's capital.

1914 — Australia enters WWI.

Index